THEORIES OF AGRICULTURAL FINANCE

Dr. V.B. Jugale

ATLANTIC
PUBLISHERS & DISTRIBUTORS (P) LTD

Published by

ATLANTIC

PUBLISHERS & DISTRIBUTORS (P) LTD

7/22, Ansari Road, Darya Ganj, New Delhi-110002
Phones : +91-11-40775252, 40775214, 23273880, 23275880
Fax: +91-11-23285873
Web: www.atlanticbooks.com
E-mail: orders@atlanticbooks.com

Printed & bound in India by Atlantic Print Services

Dedicated

To

My beloved sister

Late Sou. Sundatai Bhimrao Vader,

who encouraged and inspired me,

to learn and educate

Foreword

Agriculture even now continues to be the major economic sector of the Indian economy. On its health and proper functioning depends on the overall health of the Indian economy. A large and rapidly growing population makes it necessary to depend on agriculture for generating large number of employment opportunities. Increasing productivity, greater diversification of cropping pattern and optimum use of limited water resources along with wider and intensified introduction of modern techniques of cultivation have become essential conditions of agricultural growth. For all these purposes provision of credit at the right time, in the right quantity and at reasonable cost for agricultural purposes, assume crucial importance.

In India sincere and persistent efforts have been made by the government and banking system to meet the credit requirement of agriculture. In the last four decades we have evolved a comprehensive and a complex system of agricultural finance comprising the R.B.I., NABARD, SBI, Nationalised commercial banks, the regional rural banks and a vastly expanded system of co-operative credit. All this has certainly contributed to the increasing agricultural production and prosperity.

However, there are problems which need immediate and careful attention. One of the problems is the increasing overdues of the cooperative credit sector which has again and again compelled some of the state governments to write off significantly large amounts of agricultural loans, under the pressure from the agitating and growing agricultural lobby.

It is on this background that this book by Dr. V.B. Jugale is a timely addition to the literature on agricultural credit. Jugale has discussed the role of agriculture in economic development, the characteristics of Indian agriculture, theories of agricultural finance and in the last chapter he elaborates the concept of the co-operative village bank which, in his opinion, constitutes a remedy for many of the co-operative credit system. I congratulate Dr. V.B. Jugale on having done an excellent job on one of the aspects of his Ph.D. thesis which dealt with the problems of co-operative credit. I am confident that the readers will find this book interesting, useful and stimulating.

Dr. J.F. Patil
Deptt. of Economics,
Kolhapur

Preface

Agriculture is an activity undertaken to satisfy the basic needs of the mankind. Though dependent on nature to a great extent it depends on both man and material inputs. Credit is one of the basic inputs for agricultural growth and development. Timely, adequate and right type of credit penetrates into agriculture and injects an element of healthy competition and concrete commercial calculations in farm operations. Now-a-days "credit serves as an elevator". It no more "supports the farmers as the hangman's rope supports the hanged". Credit is essential because our farmers are poor and backward, besides agriculture is seasonal and takes months to receive the return.

Credit is a problem when it cannot be obtained and it is also a problem when it is not properly utilised. There are various types of agricultural credit being supplied by a variety of credit agencies. Agricultural finance has gradually evolved over a long time period with changing conditions but the cause has remained more or less the same, *i.e.,* either drought condition or improvidence and extravagance of the farmers.

The introduction of taquavi consequent upon the problems of farmers' indebtedness and recurrent drought conditions led to the formation of co-operative credit societies during the first decade of this century. The initial thrust of the co-operative movement was mainly in the field of agricultural credit. Today the proportion of cooperative credit borrowing is about 25 per cent, while commercial banks share is only 12 per cent in the total borrowings of agriculturists. There is wider future scope for co-operative movement to develop in the field of agricultural credit. But restructurisation of the whole co-operative credit structure is necessary, depending on the characteristics of Indian agriculture and agriculturists. Our agriculture has been characterised with different features other than observed in other countries.

The present work is a part of doctoral dissertation submitted by me to the Shivaji University, Kolhapur. Here an attempt is made to analyse certain theoretical aspects evolved in agricultural credit system. A new system in the form of CVBs is suggested as to restructure the whole co-operative movement at gross-root level. Co-operation is the only system to be adopted to develop our farm economy in particular and rural economy in general.

This book has been divided into six chapters. Chapter-I identifies the role of agriculture in our economy and characteristics of our agricultural economy. Chapter-II deals with critical study of agricultural credit, wherein the agricultural finance system operating in India has been critically reviewed. In Chapter-III a few principles of agricultural finance and some theoretical analyses have been explained with a view to identify the nature and scope of farm credit. And at last cooperative village banks (CVBs) have been suggested to restructure the Primary Agricultural Co-operative Societies (PACS) in rural areas.

It is, however, incomplete unless I express my thanks to Dr. J.F. Patil, for his continuous guidance and valuable suggestions. I am happy and grateful for his foreword to this book. I am also grateful to my wife Mrs. Yojana for her helping hand in preparing the manuscript and assisting to me in the whole work. I am also thankful to the publishers, who extended my views to the readers. At last I would like to say that I would heartily welcome any valuable comments and suggestions in writing. Shortcomings are undoubtedly authors' personal responsibility.

Dr. V.B. Jugale

Contents

1

Role and Characteristics of Indian Agriculture

1.1. Introduction

Man's struggle with nature for his existence has been incessant since time immemorial. Sometimes man is successful in overcoming the natures odds, and sometimes nature express its dreadful character. Both lay a claim over one another.

Agriculture has been the major battlefield of the initial struggle between nature and man. It is a culture that man has invented. Agriculture is also a natural science and essentially connected with human needs. Man has invented this art to satisfy his growing necessities. Agriculture though a natural science, depends on the human efforts, along with inputs of physical, material, institutional and technical kinds. Without these inputs agriculture may not be called as agriculture. Continuous growth in population has compelled further improvements in agricultural practices. Such improvements lead to an economic development and economic development in its turn, necessarily causes further improvements in agricultural sector.

Although, a country's overall development is dependent on the growth and development of agriculture and industry. In India, the agriculture sector plays a predominant role in total development. India is a vast country with a variety of resources, and agriculture as the main occupation. In rural area, where agriculture is the main practice, with 76.72 per cent of population lives in 5.65 lakhs villages; and the rest 23.27 per cent population lives in 3245 towns and cities. Agriculture helps industry and industry motivate agriculture to develop. Development cannot be achieved without industrial progress. The commercialisation of agriculture paves the way for agro-industries and which revive manufacturing activities. Both the industry and agriculture essentially need capital.

Agriculture has a very wide scope of development but very slow growth. While every country's early development was entirely dependent on agriculture, any country called developed today, was an agriculturally backward country at some time. Any developing economy has to develop agriculture first before it can be industrially developed. So, the development strategies adopted by developing economies till today and will have to be adopted, with a greater intensity in India. In developing and poverty ridden countries, development of agriculture is considered as the expansion of output. Not only this but an equal distribution of output is emphasised. "The crisis of agriculture in underdeveloped world is a silent one, only rarely does the misery of most of mankind become dramatic."[1] The developed countries also have to face drastic shortages of agricultural output at times. Agricultural crises in USSR[2] and USA[3] during 1986-87 and 1987-88 respectively exemplify this.

Since independence we have materially tried hard in terms of material inputs to develop our agriculture, but we lack in human involvement, because we have not been able to change the traditional attitude of the cultivator. Any plan of agricultural development should aim at changing the cultivator into an active partner in important decision-making on all levels of farm and business management and thus assure his participation in development planning.[4] The traditional methods of farming in India involve a combination of land, labour, animal power and a few implements for tillage, interculture, irrigation and harvest. A change in above methods was initiated during mid-sixties as "Green Revolution" in India, and all agriculture has undergone a drastic face-lift. Since then, various inputs have contributed to the overall agricultural development. Also activities both inside and outside the farm have contributed for the healthy development of agriculture. Despite this, self-reliance in food grains production is uncertain, because of various constraints that the agriculture sector faces.

Agriculture, though practised since very long years, still remains a tough task, and a hard way of living. In our country the prime objective of economic development plan is to increase the agricultural productivity, where farmers who constitute 63% of population operate a very small, cultivated area (18.80% of total land area). And the objective of the plan is to raise the farm productivity and income levels of these farmers. The pre-condition to achieve this is the transformation of subsistence agriculture into viable commercial farming. But the whole process of agricultural transformation depends upon multiplicity of factors, such as technological and institutional changes, provision of service facilities, effective extension work and so on. "Agriculture is not merely a way of making money by raising crops, it is not merely an industry or a business, it is essentially a public function or service preferred by private individuals for the care and use of the land in the national interest, and farmers in the course of their pursuit of a living and a private profit are the custodians on the basis of the national life;"[5] Not only this, the ecological problems of agricultural development cannot be isolated from those of economic development in general. The Green Revolution has brought into being some economic problems dealing with ecological issues, though it is also responsible for the socio-cultural transformation of rural scene, with visible positive and negative sides. So, the need is to assess agricultural development with reference to socio-economic and ecological life of the society bearing in mind that progress is resultant condition of nuisance at present day conditions in the way of life. A recent practice, "natural farming" innovated by Japanese wonder farmer, Masanobu Fukuoka has accepted primarily agriculture as a way of tackling the ecological imbalances occurring due to green revolution, because the ecological sustainability of the production system has not been observed all the time. But it is essential to monitor or evaluate this. The ecological balance between soil, water, genetic resources of plant, animals and fisheries etc. should be maintained. An appropriate cropping pattern should be evolved according to the region on a scientific basis with a required additional efficiency in the utilisation of inputs. That is why we are thinking of "Second Green Revolution" today. The "Second Green Revolution" should be considered proper perspective and positively involved into promoting the agrarian and rural prosperity and better quality of life in villages. So, Indian agriculture needs a new vision if further progress is to be made. The task is not easy, but it can be accomplished, if socio-political will and professional outlook can be combined. Farmers ought to occupy the pride of place in agricultural planning.

1.2. Role of Agriculture in Rural Development

As pointed out earlier, the place of agriculture in development activities is necessarily very significant.

Agriculture increases food supply, transfer of labour resources to secondary sectors, leads to additional capital formation for other important sectors, and creates additional purchasing power.[6] This sector has a greater potentiality in raising the production and creates the infrastructure for the rest of the economy. This sector has a horizontal and vertical links with the economy (See Chart-1). Agriculture "in the first place can provide workers to industry, second, it can furnish demand for industrial output, third, it can provide savings for use in industry or by Govt. in forming social overhead capital. Fourth, it may pay taxes to Govt. Fifthly, agriculture can earn foreign exchange through exports to pay for important capital equipment and raw materials needed in other sectors, sixthly, it can supply food for consumption by workers in industry and capital formation".[7]

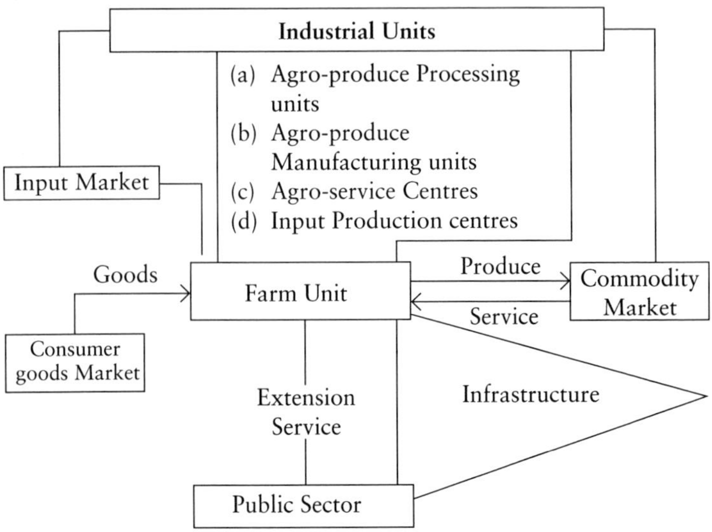

Chart No. 1.1: Share of Agriculture in Rest of the Economy

The history of development of various developed countries reveals that, there is a certain correlation between the process of overall economic development and agricultural development. At an early stage of economic development 'subsistence fund' is a very important form of 'capital good' that classical economists had emphasised. An adequate supply of food enables a country to escape from a hand to mouth existence and devote a larger amount of labour to the production of more sophisticated kinds of capital goods which increase in output. Accordingly, green revolution, it was thought, would pave the way for rapid industrial growth.[8] Isher Ahluwalia and *et-al* calculated that, "one per cent fall in agricultural income will lead to a 0.5 per cent fall in industrial income."[9] But the evidence is so overwhelming that one is tempted to make a generalisation that the overall economic development is mainly reflected in rapid industrialisation, which is invariably related to technological revolution in agriculture leading to significant and sometimes miraculous increases in agricultural productivity. Though the general tendency is to equate economic development with industrialisation, Jacob Viner argues, that, "a high degree of industrialisation is not necessary for raising the per capita income of a country. This can be achieved also by improving agriculture without having any great recourse to the development of industries. Dominantly agricultural countries are generally found to be poor, not because they are agricultural but because their agriculture is backward."

The socio-economic and cultural backwardness of our rural population kept them in a 'vicious circle' typical of underdeveloped country. Fortunately, however, "bigger and most backward the sector, the greater are the possibilities of economic development *via* agriculture."[10] In certain respects the growth of agriculture differs from the growth of rest of the economy, because of the nature and characteristics of agricultural sector, "Several characteristics of agriculture which differ in degree at least from most non-farm industries include (i) higher rate of technological change, (ii) inelastic demand for its product, (iii) the difficulty of controlling production, (iv) the "rugged individualism" of farm operations, (v) the chronic high level of unemployment of labour in some regions, and (vi) a high degree of risk and uncertainty."[11]

Since planning began in this country, agricultural outlay has shown a major share in total outlay (See table 1.1) and from the First Five Year Plan (1951-56) agricultural sector has shown a kind of development buoyancy. Table No. 1.1 reveals the fact that share of agriculture in public outlays in all plans remained constant.

Plans	Share of Agriculture:		Share of Irrigation		Total %
	Amount (Crores)	% to total outlay:	Amount (Crores)	% to total Outlays	
First F.Y.P.	354	14.8	469	22.2	37.0
Second F.Y.P.	510	11.7	402	9.2	20.9
Third F.Y.P.	1068	12.7	650	7.8	20.5
Annual Plans	1037	16.7	426	7.1	23.8
Fourth F.Y.P.	2728	14.7	1087	8.6	23.3
Fifth F.Y.P.	4766	12.3	3434	9.8	22.1
Sixth F.Y.P.	10539	13.6	12160	10.1	23.7
Seventh F.Y.P.	22793	12.6	16979	9.4	22.0

Table No. 1.1: Share of Agricultural Outlay in Total Outlays During Plan Period

Source: India: Basic Economic Information (ed.) Agarwal, Verma and Gupta, pp. 204-5.

Rural development can be achieved by assisting agriculture according to the needs of public, rational utilisation of resource, educating the farmer in modern technology, organising the income generation schemes, creating infrastructure for agro-industrial base, and credit allotment schemes for agricultural activities. Fourth Five Year Plan was largely depended on intensive agricultural growth with above strategies. Special schemes for small farmers and marginal farmers were implemented for raising the farm productivity and improving the economic conditions of small and marginal farmers. Since Fourth Five Year Plan, the planning strategy centres around the above objectives. A pre-condition for raising farm productivity and income level of small farms is transformation of their subsistence agriculture into commercial farming as mentioned earlier. It is understandable that the transformation will depend upon a multiplicity of factors such as institutional reforms, technological change, provision of credit and marketing facilities, effective extension work and so on.[12] Thus agricultural development means bringing modern technology in agriculture for growing yield, reforming organisational structure of land ownership, providing credit and other inputs at reasonable rates to improve quality of agriculture in comparison with past experience. These components of agricultural development are the components of rural development too. Both agricultural development and rural development have various components bearing not only economic aspects but also socio-cultural aspects. So, "a study of the process of agricultural development has to be comprehensive in its scope and include not only various economic aspects but some sociological ones too. This is especially so in the case of agriculture, because the economic unit (the farm) and the sociological unit (the family)are closely intertwined, mutually reacting on each other."[13] As agriculture is centralised in rural India with a large portion of population, it is not wrong to say that rural development means agricultural development, and the same to total economic development.

J.W. Mellor[14] distinguishes three phases of agricultural development: (a) traditional agriculture, (b) technologically dynamic agriculture with low capital intensity, and (c) technologically dynamic agriculture with high capital intensity. The second phase is entrusted with agriculture still representing a large proportion of the total economy, demand for agricultural products is raising rapidly due to body demographic and income effects, (c) capital for industrial development is particularly scarce and returns are raising, (d) limitations to the pace of economic transformation and pressure of population growth preclude enlargement of average acreage per farm (e) use of labour-saving agricultural machinery is largely precluded by unfavourable labour-capital cost relationship. Our agriculture has begun this stage since green revolution during mid-sixties. To some extent modernisation of agriculture is taking place which induced the farmers to invest in agriculture for profit purposes. And the expansion of secondary and tertiary sector too encourages the agriculture to invest in it. Modernisation of agriculture mean utilisation of modern techniques of inputs and farm management according to the market needs, which again is helpful to overcome the natural obstacles.

Modernisation of agriculture is greatly related to commercialisation of agriculture or industrialisation of agriculture *i.e.* looking towards it as business. Generally development is related to industrialisation. And industrialisation has a link towards socio-economic regulations in human life. Therefore, industrialisation of agriculture may be a strategy to be accepted for rural development. In a country like ours, where the resources are abundant in agricultural sector for industrialisation purposes, there, the policy towards agricultural industrialisation must be perspective and foresighted. Moreover industrialisation motivate the agriculture sector into commercialisation and *vice-versa*. During the first decade after inception of green revolution, it was not distinguished by an acceleration in industrial growth. Industry in fact, decelerated. In subsistence agriculture, most of the farm inputs are raised on the farm as agriculture moves towards progressive modernisation, the proportion of external input will tend to rise, which may result into increase in production, and the increased income will be invested again in irrigation and complementary infrastructure feasible for further agricultural development.

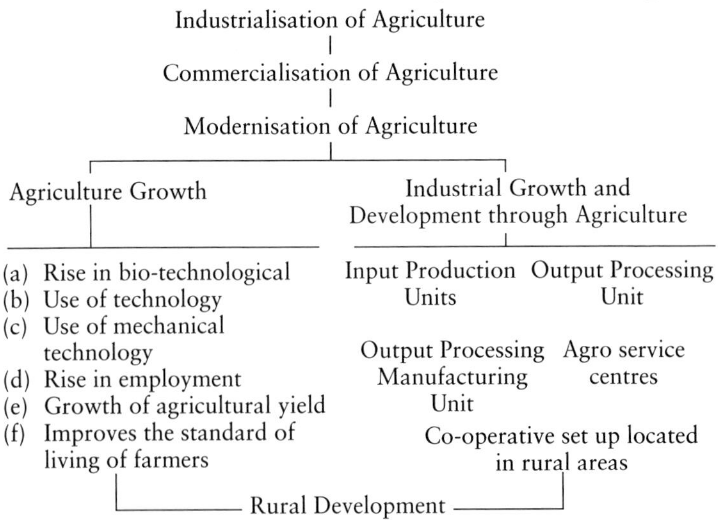

Chart No. 1.2

Thus the standard of living in rural area will improve. There is a consensus of opinion, that savings are likely to be substantially high in developed agricultural tracts, where commercial crops are grown, while in other regions there are likely to be meagre.

As suggested in chart 1.2 the industrialisation of agriculture is, therefore, essential and it is possible only when there is a fair atmosphere for industrialisation. Only one factor will not bring a change, indeed the change in human factor is the more required one. However, the required socio-political and economic atmosphere should be created for which we always look towards the Govt. But instead of looking at the Govt.'s helping hand, a rural area in particular may be developed through using the local resources in a co-operative way. Maharashtra State has shown this by way of co-operatives. The co-operatives have both vertical and horizontal links in rural economy. But one thing should be clear that all policies pertaining to rural development should centre around considering the major characteristics of our agriculture.

1.3. Characteristics of Indian Agriculture

Indian agriculture has been characterised into a variety of aspects. The sector is entrusted with some specific features, distinguishing it from other developing countries. During the old days a proper balance between agriculture and industry was observed in our economy, which continued till the middle of the 18th century. The interference of British Government throttled the whole village economy. Particularly the art of village handicrafts vanished and dependence on agriculture increased.

It was only after independence and the inception of planning era; the green revolution is possible during 1966. Since then, the whole sector has undergone a structural and phenomenal change, and made our country self-reliant in food grains production during mid-eighties. The progress can be seen in both vertical and horizontal, as well as infrastructural aspects of this core sector. Progress in agricultural education and research done in our universities is phenomenal. The input technologies have developed moderately. Various laws, rules and regulations were formulated to remove the bottlenecks for the vital development of agriculture, although the present characteristics are different from that of earlier scenario.

1.3.1. Size of Holding

The details of size of holding and the area operated by farmers is shown in Table No. 1.2 below. The average size of holding in India is small and mainly it is declining. Only the average of small holding group is constant and the area they hold is increasing. Both area of holding and number of large holdings is decreasing. While the number of holding of medium group is decreasing and the area of holding of the same group is near about same. The area of holding by small and semi-medium group is increasing though there is a decline in their number. The number and the holding of marginal size group is increasing. About 56 per cent of holdings belong to uneconomic size. However, the area and number of marginal holdings are increasing.

Size of holding (Hectares)	No. of holding (Millions)			Area of holding (Million hectares)		
	1970 -71	1976 -77	1980 -81	1970 -71	1976 -77	1980 -81
1. Marginal (MF) (Below-1)	36.20 (51.0)	44.5 (54.6)	50.52 (56.5)	14.56 (9.0)	17.5 (10.7)	19.80 (12.2)
2. Small (SF) (1-2 hectare.)	13.43 (18.9)	14.7 (18.0)	16.08 (18.0)	19.28 (11.9)	20.9 (12.8)	22.96 (14.1)
3. Semi-Medium (SmF)(2-4 hectare)	10.68 (15.0)	11.7 (14.4)	12.51 (14.0)	30.00 (18.5)	32.4 (19.8)	34.56 (21.2)
4. Medium(MdF) (4-10 hectare)	7.93 (11.2)	8.2 (10.1)	8.09 (9.1)	48.24 (29.7)	49.6 (30.4)	48.34 (29.7)
5. Large (LF) (10 and above)	2.77 (3.9)	2.4 (2.9)	2.15 (2.4)	50.06 (30.9)	42.9 (29.3)	37.13 (22.8)
Total	71.01 (100.00)	81.5 (100.00)	89.35 (100.00)	162.14 (100.00)	163.3 (100.00)	162.79 (100.00)

Table No. 1.2: Operational Holding

*The data in parenthesis indicate the percentage to the total.

The sub-division and fragmented land pieces is another character of our farming sector. The 8th round of NSS, conducted during 1954-55 envisage that, an increase in the size of holdings, the average number of fragments also increased. For example for holdings between 0.1 to 2.49 acres, the number of units was 2.89, for 2.50 to 4.49 acres, the number of units on an average was 7.09; for 5.50 to 7.49 acres, the number of units raised to 8.19 and for 7.50 to 9.99 acres the number of units reached at 8.82. Beyond that, for holding 10 to 14.99 acres the number moved further up to 9.21; for 15 to 19.99 acres the number was at 9.46 and for holding above 20 acres the number jumped further to 9.89.

1.3.2. The Falling Rate of Share of Agricultural Income in Total National Income

The share of agriculture in national income is often taken as an indicator of economic development. The share of agriculture in total national income is declining since World War I. Before that about two-third of this share belong to agriculture. Normally, such economies are called as underdeveloped economies. The share of agriculture in gross domestic products depicts the fact of our dependence on agriculture. In 1950-51 the share of agriculture in net domestic product was roughly one-half. During the same period the share of agriculture and allied activities in total national GDP at constant prices of 1970- 71 was 58.9 per cent, which fell down to 37 per cent 1984-85 (See Table 1.3). Recently the F.A.O. Regional Office for Asia and Pacific measured the share of agriculture in India's total national income at about 33 per cent, while the population engaged in farming is about 61 per cent during the end of 1987.[15]

Years	%
1950-51	58.9
1955-56	57.3
1960-61	54.2
1964-65	49.9
1968-69	46.3
1973-74	45.2
1978-79	41.6
1980-81	40.6
1984-85	37.4
1987-88 (Dec.)	33*

Table No. 1.3: Share of Agriculture and Allied Activities in Gross Domestic Product at Constant 1970-71 Prices (%)

*F.A.O. Calculation

Though our economy has been characterised as underdeveloped, the share of agriculture in total GDP is decreasing. It means the dependence on agriculture is declining, and it is a good symptom, because manufacturing and industrial sector have higher growth rate than agriculture. Western experiment shows that, the less dependence on agriculture means, better growth of the economy.

	1986-87	1985-86	1984-85	1981-82
Primary of which:	82,596 (35.8)	76,874 (37.2)	71,754 (38.9)	52,439 (40.8)
Agriculture	71,051 (30.8)	66,473 (32.1)	61,733 (33.5)	44,971 (35.0)
Mining	5832 (2.5)	5138 (2.5)	5013 (2.7)	3020 (2.4)
Secondary of which:	57,714 (25.1)	50,593 (24.4)	43,519 (23.6)	29,230 (22.8)
Manufacturing (Regd.)	26,611 (11.5)	23,401 (11.3)	19,663 (10.7)	11,779 (9.2)
Manufacturing (unregd.)	15,549 (6.7)	14,137 (6.8)	12,616 (6.8)	9964 (7.8)
Transport, Communication and Trade of which:	43,054 (18.7)	38,097 (18.4)	33,205 (18.0)	22,214 (17.3)
Railways	2432 (1.1)	1891 (0.9)	1416 (0.8)	930 (0.7)
Trade, Hotels etc.	31,021 (13.5)	28,142 (13.6)	24,750 (13.4)	17,563 (13.7)
Finance and Real Estates of which:	18,502 (8.0)	16,898 (8.2)	14,865 (8.1)	10,709 (8.3)
Banking and Insurance	9402 (4.1)	8364 (4.0)	7070 (3.8)	4488 (3.5)
Community, Social and Personal services of which:	28,598 (12.4)	24,403 (11.8)	21,132 (11.5)	13,825 (10.8)
Public adm. and Defence	13,472 (5.8)	11,099 (5.4)	9814 (5.3)	6070 (4.7)
Total:	2,30,464 (100.0)	2,06,865 (100.0)	1,84,475 (100.0)	1,28,417 (100.0)

Table No. 1.4: Net Domestic Product by Industry of Origin (New Series: Current prices)*

(₹ Crores)

Note: Figures in brackets show percentage to total' *Provisional.
Source: Tata Services Ltd., Deptt. of Economics and Statistics, 1988-89.

According to Egbert de Vries, for every 10 per cent increase in per capita real income, the fraction of national income arising from agriculture declines by 1.5 per cent points.[16] In India, about 10 to 15 per cent share of agriculture in total national income has declined during the period between 1951-1987. Particularly the decline of share of agriculture since the beginning of this decade is high. At the end of this century it will fall between 20 to 25 per cent. Table 1.4 illustrates the net domestic product by industry of origin at current prices. The fact that agriculture still contribute more than one-third of the net domestic income shows its significant role in Indian economy. This can be understood clearly if we notice that the share of agriculture in U.S.A. is only 3 per cent.

If we consider the current prices of agricultural output, we observe that the prices of output have grown less than input prices since independence. The Central Statistical Organisation has brought this out by estimating and comparing the actual and net income from agriculture (after deducting the cost of inputs and consumption of fixed capital) in 1970-71 and 1983-84. The best agricultural year so far, 1983-84, has been chosen for comparison so that weather observations may not be blamed for the deteriorating economic condition of farmers as Table 1.5 below reveals:[17]

		1970-71	1983-84	%change
1.	(1) Value of farm output at current prices (₹ crores)	20729	78026	276.4
2.	Less inputs and consumption of fixed capital at current prices (₹ crores)	4512	22655	402.1
3.	Net income accruing at current prices (₹ crores) at	16217	55371	241.4
	1970-71 prices	16217	17522*	8.0
4.	Population dependent on agriculture (Million)	360	480	33.0
5.	Per-capita income at 1970-71 prices (₹)	450.5	365.0	–19.0
6.	Index of farm production	111.5	156.4	403

Table No. 1.5: Per Capita Real Income from Agriculture

*Obtained by dividing the net income at current prices by 3.16 the income multifile for 1983-84.

The table 1.5 reveals the fact that about 40 per cent of increase in agricultural production is seen, but the total net income from agriculture (1970-71 prices) has increased by only 8 per cent, and if the increase in population dependent on agriculture is considered, the PCI declined by about 19 per cent. This is mainly due to the faster rise in prices of farm inputs, as compared to those of the output.[18] According to the "Research Highlight — 1986-87" published by the Union Ministry of Agriculture, "prices of farm inputs have increased 235 times faster than those of farm outputs."[19] If we compare the whole-sale price index (at 1970-71) of food grains and industrial products it would be 333 per cent and 415 per cent respectively. There is about 25 per cent difference between the two. If the PCI from agriculture is assumed at rupee one, then the PCI from industrial sector will be at ₹ 3.64. The problem will not be solved if we increase the prices of food grains. If this is done problems too serious to tackle will ensure.

1.3.3. The Falling Rate of Share of Agriculture in Total Population

Indian occupational structure is the best example of an underdeveloped economy. Majority of Indian population is engaged in agriculture sector. However, a trend of declining rate of population is seen (See Table 1.6). Particularly during 1971-81 decades, there is a decline of about 4 per cent.

The percentage of agricultural labour is increasing, in which the percentage of female agricultural labourers is high (28.60%) during 1961-71, however this declined to 5.29 per cent between 1971-81, while the percentage of female cultivators increased by 3.3 per cent during 1971-81. A favourable growth of industrial sector is held responsible in minimising the percentage involvement-of population in agriculture sector. In developed countries the population percentage belonging to agriculture sector is very small. In U.S.A. it is about only 4 per cent and in U.K. 3 per cent population belongs to agriculture. Immediately after World War II, nearly 50 per cent (7.20 crores) of Japanese population was engaged in agriculture, today only about 11 per cent (1.30 crores) population belong to agriculture. Even in socialist countries this percentage is also small. In the U.S.S.R. during 1965, about 34 per cent of population belonged to agriculture, and today this percentage is about 18 (1985).

According to 1981 census, 68.7 per cent of population belongs to agriculture sector. As recently estimated by FAO

(1987, Dec.) about 61 per cent of Indian population belongs to agriculture. There is a regional variation in occupational structure of population. In the states where agriculture is important and growing rapidly (Punjab, Madhya Pradesh, Kerala, Maharashtra) the share of agriculture in work-force has decreased. And in the states (Uttar Pradesh, Rajasthan, Assam, Orissa) where agriculture is important but stagnant the share of agriculture in the work-force has increased.

Sector and industrial categories	1901	1911	1921	1931	1951	1961	1971	1981
1. Agricultural Sector	71.7	74.9	76.0	74.8	72.1	71.8	72.1	68.7
a) Cultivators	50.6	49.8	54.4	54.1	50.0	52.1	43.4	41.6
b) Agri. labour	16.9	20.6	17.6	24.8	16.7	26.7	26.3	24.9
c) Livestock, forestry, fishing etc.	4.2	4.5	4.2	4.9	2.6	2.3	2.4	2.2
2. Industrial Sector	12.6	11.1	10.5	10.2	10.7	12.2	11.2	13.5
a) Mining and quarrying	0.1	0.2	03	.03	0.6	0.5	0.5	0.6
b) Large and small industries	11.7	9.0	9.3	8.9	9.0	10.6	9.5	113
c) Construction	0.8	1.0	0.9	1.0	1.1	1.1	1.2	1.6
3. Service Sector	15.7	14.0	13.5	15.0	17.2	16.0	16.7	17.8
a) Trade and Comm.	6.1	5.5	5.7	5.6	5.2	4.0	5.6	63
b) Trans. Storage Communications	1.1	1.1	0.9	1.0	1.5	1.6	2.4	2.7
4. Other services	8.5	7.4	6.9	8.4	10.5	10.4	8.7	83
Total:	100	100	100	100	100	100	100	100

Table No. 1.6: Occupational Distribution of Working Population (%)

1.3.4. Availability of Food Production

The initial agricultural policies emphasised on "grow more food" because of the severe shortage of food supply. About two-thirds of total agricultural production was related to food grains. The most important component in the food grains category was rice, followed by wheat. Even today the same percentage with a little variation is continued. Table 1.7 reveals the fact that after the Third Plan period, *i.e.*, the period of green revolution, rapid strides in rice, wheat, jowar, bajra and maize has been seen.

Plan Period	Rice	Wheat	Jowar	Bajra	Maize	Other Cereals	Pulses	Total food-grains
1950-51	20.6 (40.55)	6.4 (12.59)	5.5 (10.82)	2.6 (5.11)	1.7 (3.34)	6.1 (12)	8.4 (16.53)	50.8 (100.0)
1st Plan	25.0 (39.55)	7.9 (12.5)	7.5 (11.86)	3.4 (5.37)	2.7 (4.27)	6.6 (10.44)	10.1 (15.98)	63.2 (100.0)
2nd Plan	30.3 (40.94)	9.7 (13.10)	8.7 (11.75)	3.4 (4.59)	3.6 (4.86)	65 (8.78)	11.7 (15.81)	74.0 (100.0)
3rd Plan	35.1 (43.33)	11.1 (13.70)	8.8 (10.86)	3.9 (4.81)	4.6 (5.67)	6.3 (7.77)	11.1 (13.70)	81.0 (100.0)
Annual Plans	35.9 (40.80)	15.5 (17.65)	9.7 (11.04)	45 (512)	5.6 (6.37)	6.2 (7.06)	103 (11.73)	87.8 (100.0)
4th Plan	41.8 (40.58)	23.4 (22.71)	83 (8.05)	6.0 (5.82)	6.1 (5.92)	6.4 (6.21)	10.9 (10.58)	103.0 (100.0)
5th Plan	47.3 (40.05)	29.8 (25.23)	103 (9.14)	5.0 (4.23)	6.3 (5.33)	71 (6.01)	11.7 (9.90)	118.1 (100.0)
1980-81	53.6 (41.35)	36.3 (28.0)	10.4 (8.02)	53 (4.08)	7.0 (5.40)	63 (4.86)	10.6 (8.17)	129.6 (100.0)
1983-84	60.1 (39.43)	45.5 (29.85)	11.9 (7.80)	7.7 (5.05)	7.9 (5.18)	6.4 (4.19)	12.9 (8.46)	152.4 (100.0)
1984-85	58.6 (40.08)	44.2 (30.23)	11.2 (7.66)	6.2 (4.24)	8.4 (5.74)	5.4 (3.69)	12.2 (8.34)	146.2 (100.0)

Table No. 1.7: Trends in Food Productions (Million tonnes)

* Figures in parenthesis indicate % to total.

But the per-capita availability of food grains is declining year after year (See table 1.8). The total food grain production during 1986-87 constituted about 144.07 million tonnes, and during 1987-88, it was expected that the total food grains production would be about 138.4 million tonnes. And during 1989 and 2000 A.D. it is projected between 166 and 170 million tonnes and between 230 to 250 million tonnes respectively. Table 1.8 illustrates that the per capita availability of food grains per day is declining since pre-independence period. This is because of two factors: (a) rise in population, (b) frequent drought condition in major parts of the country. Because of this reason our import of food grains is yet not stopped. In 1983-94 we imported 2470 thousand tonnes of food grains. Particularly during 1981-82 and 1983-84 the import increased more than usual.

Pre-independence period		Post-independence period	
Period (Quinquennium ending)	Grams Per day	Period (Quinquennium ending)	Grams Per day
1905-6	549	1956	431
1910-11	543	1961	469
1915-16	525	1965	480
1920-21	534	1970	455
1925-26	549	1975	406
1930-31	493	1980	411
1935-36	467	1985	454
1940-41	434	1986	476
1945-46	417	1987	466

Table No. 1.8: Per capita Availability of Food grains Per-day – 1905-1987

1.3.5. Dependence of Nature

Since the Green Revolution, we have doubled the net area under irrigation. However only about 25 per cent of cropped area (grossly 32.71%) comes under the net irrigated area, which was only 16.16 per cent (grossly 18.3%) in 1960-61.

The trend of rainfall during south-western monsoon shows a decline from the normal rainfall (see Table 1.9) during a few years

Departure Class	No. of Years
0 to + 5	28
+ 5 to + 10	22
+ 10 to + 15	5
+ 15 to + 20	7
> + 20	2
0 to – 5	19
– 5 to – 10	11
– 10 to – 15	8
– 15 to – 20	3
> – 20	4

Table No. 1.9: Departure of Monsoon Rainfall in % India* (1875 to 1984)

Source: Why monsoon fail, P.K. Das, Scientific Reporter (CSIR), May 1988

States	Net sown Area (000 he)	Ultimate irrigation, potential (Gross) (000he)	Gross irrigated Area (000he)	% of irrigated Potential not utilised(Col (4÷3)–1	Net irrigated Area (000he)	NIA/ GIA	% of 1983-84 NSA Dependent on Rainfall(1)
Andhra Pradesh	11436	9200	5058	45.0	3878	0.7667	38.32
Assam	2696	2670	572	78.6	572	1.0000	0.96
Bihar	7580	12400	3570	71.2	2517	0.7050	-15.33(2)
Gujarat	9583	4750	2614	45.0	2240	0.8569	57.53
Haryana	3600	4550	3594	21.0	2190	0.6093	22.99
Himachal Pradesh	593	335	165	50.7	94	0.5700	67.80
Jammu-Kashmir	729	800	413	48.4	321	0.7772	14.71
Karnataka	10605	4600	1945	57.7	1590	0.8175	64.54
Kerala	2180	2100	396	81.1	266	0.6717	32.29
Madhya Pradesh	19223	10200	2867	71.9	2772	0.9669	48.49
Maharashtra	18302	7300	2686	63.2	1964	0.7312	70.84
Orissa	5990	5900	2006	66.0	1845	0.9697	9.41
Punjab	4212	6550	6273	4.2	3609	0.5753	10.54
Rajasthan	16324	5150	4014	22.1	3276	0.8161	74.25
Tamil Nādu	5846	3900	3249	16.7	2618	0.8058	46.24
Uttar Pradesh	17273	25700	12148	52.7	9879	0.8132	-20.99(2)
West Bengal	5341	6100	1980	67.5	1980	1.000	-14.21(2)
All India	142744	113402	53937	52.4	41955	0.7779	38.20

Table No. 1.10: Irrigation Potential and Dependence on Rainfall in 1983-84

Notes: 1. This relates to the proportion of net sown area that would remain entirely dependent on rain even when the irrigation potential is fully utilised at the irrigation intensity implied by the ratio of net to gross irrigated area observed in 1983-84 *i.e.* (Col. 7 × Col. 3/ Col. 2) – 1.

2. Negative values indicate that utilisation of the irrigation potential will more than cover the 1983-84 NSA at the 1983-84 level of irrigation intensity (NIA/GIA)

Source: 1. Seventh Five Year Plan.

2. Indian Agricultural Statistics. Quoted in Prospects of Enhancing Labour Productivity in Indian Agriculture — S. Mahendra Dev. EPW, Sept. 24th, 1988, P.A-108.

	1983-84	1982-83*	1980-81	1970-71
		(Million hectares)		
Source-wise				
Govt. Canals	15.7 (37.5)	14.8 (37.1)	14.5 (37.4)	12.0 (38.5)
Pvt. Canals	0.5 (1.2)	0.5 (1.3)	0.8 (2.1)	0.9 (2.9)
Tanks	3.8 (9.0)	3.1 (7.8)	3.2 (8.3)	4.1 (13.1)
Wells and Tubewells	19.5 (46.5)	19.1 (47.8)	17.7 (45.5)	11.9 (38.1)
Others	2.4 (5.7)	2.4 (6.0)	2.6 (6.7)	2.3 (7.3)
Total net irrigated area	**42.0**	**39.9**	**38.8**	**31.2**
Crops-wise	(100.0)	(100.0)	(100.00)	(100.00)
Rice	17.4 (32.3)	16.1 (30.9)	163 (33.0)	14.4 (37.5)
Wheat	17.9 (33.2)	17.1 (32.8)	15.5 (31.3)	9.9 (26.0)
Sugarcane	2.6 (4.8)	2.8 (5.4)	2.3 (4.6)	1.9 (4.9)
Til Seeds	3.1 (5.7)	2.6 (4.9)	23 (4.6)	1.1 (2.9)
Cotton	2.3 (4.2)	2.3 (4.5)	2.1 (43)	1.4 (3.6)
Others	10.7 (19.8)	11.1 (21.5)	11.1 (22.2)	9.5 (25.1)
Total Gross	**53.9** (100.0)	**52.0** (100.0)	**49.6** (100.0)	**38.2** (100.0)

Table No. 1.11: Area Irrigated by Sources and Crops

Note: Figures in bracket show % to total irrigated area.

*Provisional

Source: Statistical outline of India—1988-89, Tata Services Ltd., p. 59.

1961, 1963, 1970, 1975, 1982) the rainfall stood above the normal rainfall rate. Although on an average about 10 to 40 per cent of the total rainfall is unutilised, and along with it goes about 8.4 million tonnes of nutrients (nitrogen, phosphorus and potash)[20]

Table 1.10 reveals the fact that about 38.20 per cent of net sown area (NSA) was dependent on rainfall. Whereas 52.4 per cent of irrigation potential was not utilised during 1983-84. It means our irrigation efficiency is critical Moreover, we lose certain cultivable area due to salinity and alkalinity every year.

The most significant sources of irrigations like wells, tube-wells and Govt. canals stood highest in comparison with other sources of irrigation. They constitute about 84 per cent in total irrigation sources available so for. (See Table 1.11). Out of total water sources wheat and rice crops harnessed about 65.5 per cent of irrigation water during 1983-84.

1.3.6. Growing Agricultural Costs

A debate on inter-sectoral terms of trade has been a much discussed topic for ever a decade. Terms of trade should be defined as the comparison of prices of exports of one sector with the other of imports from the other sector.

$$Px / Pm$$

Where: **Px** = Prices of exports
Pm = Prices of imports

Table 1.12 reveals the fact that the prices of manufactures as compared to the prices of agricultural commodities remained less during 1963-64 to 1970-71, which indicate the prices have been in favour of agricultural commodities. The period 1971-72 to 1984-85 gives the opposite results.

The leaders of farming community always criticise the growing costs of production of agricultural commodities. And it is true that the farm input prices are higher than farm outputs. According to "Research Highlights: 1986-87" published by the Union Ministry of agriculture, "price of farm inputs has increased 2.35 times faster than those of farm output", which results into the spiral decline in economic condition of agriculturists, decline in land investment, decline in productivity and decline in income at last. So the shrinkage continues.

Besides the prices of basic needs apart from agriculture are also increasing tremendously. Table 1.13 shows the increasing divergence between the procurement price of wheat and the cost of living of agricultural worker in villages (which may be assumed to be the cost of living of the majority in villages).

The procurement prices of wheat, as fixed by the Govt. has not kept pace even with the cost of living of *the Poorest* in villages."[21]

Year	General index of wholesale prices	Index manufactured products	Index agricultural commodities	Price of manufactures as % of the prices of agri. commodities
1	2	3	4	5
Base Year Weight	100.0	(29.0)	(46.1)	
1950-51	118.8	101.8	110.0	92.5
1955-56	92.5	99.6	88.0	113.2
1956-57	105.3	105.6	104.5	101.1
1957-58	108.4	108.2	107.4	100.7
1958-59	112.9	108.1	114.0	943
1959-60	117.1	11.13	116.5	95.5
1960-61	124.9	122.8	123.8	99.2
1961-62	125.1	124.6	122.9	101.4
Base Year Weight	(100.0)	(32.30)	(33.2)	
1962-63	103.8	103.2	102.3	100.9
1963-64	110.2	105.9	108.4	97.7
1964-65	122.3	109.4	130.9	83.6
1965-66	131.6	117.0	141.7	82.6
1966-67	149.9	125.3	166.6	75.2
1967-68	167.3	129.1	188.2	68.6
1968-69	165.4	132.8	179.4	74.0
1969-70	171.6	139.7	194.8	71.7
1970-71	181.1	149.7	201.4	74.3
Base Year	(100.0)	(49.87)	(40.4)	
1971-72	105.6	109.5	100.4	109.1
1972-73	116.2	121.9	110.3	110.5
1973-74	139.7	139.5	139.2	100.2
1974-75	174.9	168.8	165.9	99.3
1975-76	173.0	171.2	157.3	108.8
1976-77	176.4	175.1	158.4	110.5
1977-78	185.8	179.2	174.8	102.5
1978-79	1853	179.5	171.9	104.4
1979-80	217.6	2153	188.7	114.4
1980-81	257.3	257.3	210.5	122.2
1981-82	281.3	270.6	236.5	114.4
1982-83	288.7	272.1	248.3	109.6

—*contd.*

1	2	3	4	5
1983-84	316.0	295.8	282.8	104.6
1984-85	338.4	319.5	303.2	105.4

Table No. 1.12: Index Numbers of Wholesale Prices: Relative Prices of Manufactures and Agricultural Commodities

Source: Data in Col. 2, 3, 4 for the period 1950-51 to 1976-77 have been taken from S.L. Shetty, 'Structural Retrogression in Indian Economy' EPW (Special Supplement) 1978. Data in the same columns for the period 1977-78 to 1984-85 have been taken from Economic Survey, 1985-86, Table 5.4, p. 156. Figures in Col. 5 have been obtained by dividing figures in Col 3 by corresponding figures in Col. 4. Quoted in Misra and Puri, Indian Economy, Himalaya Pub. 1986, p. 551.

Years	Cost of living index for agricultural workers adjusted to 1970-71 = 100	Indices of procurement price of wheat (1970-71 = 100)
1979-80	187.5	151.3
1980-81	213.0	153.9
1981-82	233.3	167.1
1982-83	250.5	171.1
1983-84	271.9	186.8
1984-85	273.4	200.0
1985-86	289.1	206.6
1986-87	301.0	213.2
1987-88	320.3	218.4

Table No. 1.13: Cost of Living and Wheat Procurement Price

Source: Bhanu Pratap Singh — Do Farmers Get a Fair Deal? The Hindu Survey of Agriculture 1988, p. 17.

No doubt there should be compatibility between industry and agriculture sectors. But increasing agricultural prices is no solution, because agricultural prices can also affect the levels of output in other sectors due to forward and backward linkages. Thus the difference between India and Bharat is because of the slow rise of agricultural prices, and quick price rise in industry and manufacturing sectors. To bring the purity between Bharat and India, the prices should be fixed on the basis of cost of production. However, the cost data differs from farmer to farmer, region to region and crop to crop; which makes cost-based pricing complicated. Though complicated an adequate methodology must be evolved to bring it into practice.

1.3.7. Problems of Green Revolution

During the period of Mid-sixties Normal Barlang and his associates succeeded in finding a new variety of wheat for high yield; and the same was followed by India. A team of experts (Ford Foundation) was called to suggest ways and means to increase production and productivity of land. It gave for reaching suggestions for agricultural growth. The year 1988 was the 20th anniversary of "Green Revolution" (termed by Dr. William Gadd of U.S. Deptt of Agriculture). It was a miracle in the field of production of agricultural yield during 1968 in India; through which we could produce the world's highest yield of rice, wheat rotation in a year up to 6.7 tonnes per hectare. The production and productivity of land has increased tremendously. The use of agricultural inputs like fertilizers, high yield varieties of seeds, pesticides, irrigation sources and technical changes have contributed to the satisfactory yield from agriculture sector. Side by side the rural infrastructural facilities provided during the post-independence period are also held responsible to increase the agricultural production. The HYV programme have contributed a lot of varieties to our national growth and development. Although the declining per capita, per day availability of food grains (both pulses and cereals) continues since then. We succeeded in achieving the targets of certain crops. For example wheat production had gone up to well over 42 million tonnes by 1983 while it was projected to 42 million tonnes by 1985. But the situation is not satisfactory. Now-a-days there is stagnation in agricultural yield. We will have to produce 230 to 250 million tonnes of food grains annually by the year 2000. Dr. Swaminathan[22] has narrated the fact that, "the Green Revolution in Punjab is not a miracle. It happened only because, the following pre-requisites for its success existed in the mid-sixties: (a) land consolidation and levelling, (b) owner cultivation resulting in a long-term stake in land, (c) rural communication, (d) rural electrification, and (e) a dynamic agricultural University".

Various studies though *encomium,* the green revolution results, but also turn up the nose at its results, because:

(i) No significant improvements are seen on the per capita net availability of food grains per day (According to

Economic Survey 1985-86, the per capita net availability of cereals per day was 360.4 grams in 1956, 418.5 grams in 1965 and 424.4 grams in 1985). As far as pulses are concerned the availability has declined consistently from 70.3 grams (1956) to 61.6 grams (1965) and 38.9 grams during the same period. It was 430.7 grams in 1956, grains in 1965, 477.9 grams in 1984 and 463.3 grams in 1985.

(ii) The spread of green revolution has remained limited to a few regions of the country. Specially in Punjab, Haryana, Western U.P. and some parts of Maharashtra etc.

(iii) Large farmers have benefited more from the green revolution. The movement is held responsible to bring in inequality among rural classes. Various studies have emphasised the emergence of class conflict in rural area. The capitalist peasantry class is the outcome of green revolution and the position of workers has worsened; only the large farmers group is entrusted with modern techniques of agricultural practices.

(iv) The economic benefit from high-yielding crops motivated the farmers to send their children for education instead of using them in farming activities. After their education they could not get job opportunities in any sector other than agriculture. And, therefore, they could neither work in farm nor could they get any other job opportunities. So, there is frustration in this class. And the farmers are full of remorse, about their children's education. This situation is the result of the fact that both our education system and parents are unable to teach dignity of labour. Dr. Swaminathan has remarked that, "unless, about 200 million additional jobs are found in the off-form sectors in the rural areas in the next 12 years, the earning capacity of rural families will be low and millions of landless men and women will continue to perform unskilled jobs and will have to seek working in urban area."[23]

1.3.8. Farm Mechanism

Farm mechanism is of the major constraint because of the small size of holding in India. About 33 per cent of the total number of operational holding is less than 0.5 hectare; while 22.4 per cent of the cultivated area is accounted for by holding between 5 and 10 hectares. Farm mechanisation may be defined as utilisation of improved tools and implements, tractors, combines, pumps and the other equipment for higher production. It may not replace the manpower, indeed it increases the employment through: (a) production of implements (plastic, wooden, iron and steel), (b) repairing centres and workshops, (c) innovation activities undertaken in mechanisation centre.

Although mechanisation depends on various factors like liberal bank credit, irrigation, supply of chemical fertilizers, power, large farmers, land slope, roads etc. The use of both bio-technology and mechanical technology together should be considered with each. Mechanisation improves the human productivity and reduces drudgery considerably. The expert working group constituted by the Central Institute of Agricultural Engineering (CIAE), Bhopal in Sept. 1984 made the following observations in respect of productivity as influenced by mechanisation. The panel said, it was possible to achieve:

(a) 5 to 10 per cent improvement in yields by proper and timely seed-bed preparation.
(b) 10 to 20 per cent improvement in yields by using seed-cum- fertilizer drills.
(c) 5 to 30 per cent improvement in yields through control of weeds by use of interculture tools, sprayers and dusters.
(d) 4 to 5 per cent saving through timely and efficient harvesting and threshing operations.[24]

Farm mechanisation means not only the use of tools and techniques in the farm, but it also include the processing, storage and transport of agricultural yield.

The level of mechanisation in India is low as compared to developed countries. However, in irrigated area, mechanisation has been introduced in the farming system, through tillage by tractor and its accessories, irrigation (surface, drip and sprinkling) plant protection measures, threshing, transport, processing and procurement etc. But a rainfed mechanisation technology should have to be developed separately. The regional imbalance in using mechanical technology should improve and moreover, it should help in using the empty farm hands. Thus we should have our own mechanical technology developed on the Indian agricultural background irrespective of imported techniques from western countries.

1.3.9. *Farm Management Problems*

Now-a-days, agriculture is called as a business, and business involved risk and uncertainty. Risk and uncertainty maintenance activity which is recently developed, is called management science. Management science has been developed in various activities of industrial sphere *e.g.* marketing, financial, advertising, sales, personnel, purchase etc., agriculture too has to adopt scientific management techniques of different nature for higher production and ecological balance. The use of water, chemical fertilizers, pesticides, tillage, seedling, harvesting of agricultural activities require scientific management. Mismanagement may endanger the existence of agricultural practices.

Farm-management also include the production of sufficient food grains for growing population, fodder for livestock and raw-material to industrial activities. It is required to use the natural resources like soil, water, rain, flora and fauna, atmosphere in an efficient manner, that is according to farm management science which is a rather difficult task, because our farmers are illiterate and traditional. Such farmers always oppose or are reluctant to practice modern farm management techniques due to variety of causes. And the next generation of farmers is also reluctant to practise agriculture. So, the farm management is a major task before our agricultural planners.

A major constraint in increasing crop yields is the supply of nutrients, nitrogen in particular. India produced an estimated 5.4 million tonnes of nitrogen fertilizer in 1986-87 and imported another 1.1 million tonnes.

The cost of such nitrates is also high. So, the use of bio-fertilizers instead of chemical one will be helpful to our agriculture. A proper crop rotation and crop combination also affects the presence of nitrates in a soil. We have a tradition of

Rhizobium technology in farming activity, which yields better, healthy and nutrient crops too.

India has made tremendous growth in consumption and production of fertilizers. "The consumption of fertilizer nutrients in 1966-67 was 1.1 million tonnes with food grains production at 74.2 million tonnes. These significantly increased to 8.74 million tonnes and 144.1 million tonnes respectively in 1986-87 in spite of a widespread drought in the later year. The projected food grains production targets for 2000 A.D. with a population of about one billion is 225-245 million tonnes. When the population is expected to stabilise around 1.5 billion in 2050 A.D., 380-400 million tonnes will have to be produced to meet their requirements. To meet these targets the fertilizer nutrient requirements are estimated at 20 to 40 million tonnes respectively."[25]

Lack of integrated plant protection approach is another character of our agriculture. The use of HYVF crops necessarily require crop protection measures. The indigenous pattern of crops has vanished in some parts and is vanishing from some other parts as a result, S. Jayaraj[26] has estimated, the annual loss inflicted by pests, diseases and weeds in India is at ₹ 6000 to 7000 crores. Though there are several tactics in integrated pest management (IPM), the most common one is chemical control The total consumption of pesticides has risen to 90,000 tonnes in 1935 and is expected to cross two lakh tonnes in 2000 A.D. About 58 per cent cropped area (which comes under cereals/ millets, oilseeds and pulses) receive only 6 to 7 per cent of total pesticides, while 32 per cent of cropped area (shared by cotton 5%, rice 24% and vegetables and fruits 3%) receive 82-87 per cent of pesticides, the share of cotton in this is 52-55 per cent.[27] The use of BHC and DDT is common today. However, agronomic practices concerned with cultural, mechanical, physical and biological techniques should have to be adopted. But the question is — Can our farmers sustain such practices?

1.3.10. Subsidiary Activities

Agriculture is the only sector, which has a variety of subsidiary activities like dairy, poultry, bee-keeping, horticulture, sericulture, aquaculture, agro-industrial activities (both small and large), biogas, processing of both cash and food crops etc. And therefore, we should look towards agriculture as a business section. But due to a variety of reasons such subsidiary activities are not significantly practised on a business line. Our farmers are traditionally habituated to practise such subsidiary activities, which are essential for their family needs. We have vast opportunities to undertake agro-industrial activities such as: (a) agro-produce processing units, (b) agro-produce manufacturing units, (c) agro-inputs manufacturing units, and (d) agroservice centres etc. To develop such business attitudes among them we must launch a motivation campaign with the required supply of capital, credit, and training facilities. The MF and SF group of farmers generally practise the dairy activity. This is because of the growth of dairy societies in the villages.

Co-operative principles vitally guide and motivate to develop the subsidiary and by-product processing activities on an economic ground. But such development is very low and are located in certain states and regions of the country.

1.3.11. Farm Subsidies

Subsidy to farming sector is a mere farce, in India, "Subsidy to the farm sector" has been given a totally different meaning from what is understood by it elsewhere in the world. Subsidy for the farm sector Is the money paid to farmers in excess of what they would get. If they were exposed to free internal and external trade conditions. Therefore, in assessing the quantum of subsidy comparison is made between the domestic price of any commodity and its imported price, *i.e.* cost including freight. If the domestic price is more than the imported price producers of that commodity are said to be subsidised and the level of subsidy is indicated by the price difference."[28] The major portion of subsidy goes to the fertilizers, food, irrigation and power supplying agents, by way of payment to make good and losses suffered by such industries and government departments in supplying their inputs and services to farmers. Table 1.14 below illustrates the growing value of fertilizer subsidy incurred during 1981-32 to 1988-89.

Year	Irrigation Subsidy (in 10 million)	Electricity* Subsidy (in million)	Fertilizer Subsidy (in crores)	Credit Subsidy (in million)
1981-82	₹5234	₹4261	₹375	₹7517
1982-83	₹5826	₹6116	₹605	₹8513
1983-84	₹6474	₹7281	₹1042	₹10219
1984-35	₹6944	₹9414	₹1929	₹12180
1985-86	₹7659	₹11568	₹1923	₹14139
1986-87	₹8439	₹14570	₹1893	₹16414
1987-88	NA	NA	₹2210 BE	NA
1988-89	NA	NA	₹3000 BE	NA
1988-89	NA	NA	₹3250 RE	NA
1989-90	NA	NA	₹3651 BE	NA

Table No. 1.14: Subsidy

*18 Slates total only.

Even then our farmers have to buy at higher prices in comparison with other countries of the world. Asian Development Review[29] had brought the prices of one kilogram nitrogen bought by paying wheat and paddy both al world and Indian levels.

Table 1.15 indicates the fact that, Indians, have to sell considerably more of their wheat and paddy to buy nitrogen, in case of paddy the prices are rising while the Indian rates are declining, but they stood higher than world prices.

	1980	1981	1982	1983	1984	1985
Wheat						
At world commodity prices	2.53	2.38	2.08	1.73	2.25	2.01
At Indian prices	3.72	3.93	3.60	3.09	3.07	2.97
Paddy						
At world commodity prices	1.64	1.43	1.73	1.53	2.18	2.01
At Indian prices	4.58	4.87	4.44	3.54	3.42	3.41

Table No. 1.15: Quantity (Kg) of Grain Required to Buy 1 Kg. of Nitrogen

Source: Asian Development Review, Vol. 5, No. 1 Commodity Prices and "Fertilizer New" Quoted in, Bhanu Pratap Singh, Do farmers get a fair deal? The Hindu Survey of Agriculture 1988, p. 19.

To sum up, subsidy should reach the final beneficiaries like subsidies paid to SF, MF under rural development programmes and financial aid given to SC and ST beneficiaries in India. Majority of poor farmers are deprived of such subsidies.

1.3.12. Green Revolution to Red Revolution

Green revolution, no doubts, has provided a major incentive to rich peasant class. It is held responsible to increase the interpersonal inequalities. A rich peasantry came in light through green revolution is indulging in the political activities. To some extent they succeeded. While the number of SF, MF farmers and agricultural labour are left in the same status, where they were for four decades. The co-operative movement has strengthened both economic and political power of this rich peasant class.

The unorganised agricultural labour, MF and SF size group is inactive for a few decades. Many of them are still unable to eke out a minimum living. Recently when the prices of inputs are rising higher than that of output prices, the peasant class come forward to put their grievances through their leaders. A new leadership has emerged to activate the whole agriculturists' class against unprofitable agriculture. But the MF and SF classes of farmers and agricultural labour classes are still unorganised. There is no change in their lifestyle. Indeed their standard of living is falling due to rising price levels and declining rates of real wages. So. a kind of inarticulate conflict between labour and capitalist peasantry may emerge, but the conflict turned towards govt. There is a clear case for a new form of revolution, but any direct confrontation is avoided so far.

Notes and References

1. Griffins Keith — The Political Economy of Agrarian Change: An Essay on the Green Revolution, MacMillan, 1974, p. 2
2. Hedlund Stefan Crisis in Soviet Agriculture.
3. Shinde Annasaheb — Seti Va Pani Niyojan Va Dharanasambandhiche Kanhi Prashna (Marathi).
4. Sec, Jacob Erich H., Institutional Planning, a part of Agricultural Planning, IJAE April-June, 1964.
5. Quoted by Central Banking Enquiry Committee Report, Vol. I, Part-I, p. 48- 49 from Businessman's Commission on Agriculture
6. Johnston B.F. and Mellor J.W. —The Role of Agriculture in Economic Development, A.E.R. 4(4) 589-93, Sept. 1961.
7. Kindleberger C.P. — Economic Development, p. 218.
8. Sau Ranjit — The Green Revolution and Industrial Growth in India: A tale of two paradoxes and a half EPW, Vol. XXIII, No. 16, 1988, p. 789.

9. EPW Nov., 28, 1987, p. 2043.
10. Daniel A.V. — Strategy for Agricultural Development, p.8
11. Baum, Diesslin, Heady (ed) — Capital and Credit Need in Changing Agriculture, p. 3.
12. Parikh, Goku — Alleviating the Suffering of Small Farmers, Khadi Gramodyog, May, 1972, p. 143.
13. IJAE — Conditions of Economic Progress of Farmers: An analysis of thirty-six case studies, 1960, p. 1.
14. Mellor J.S. — The Economics of Agricultural Development, Cornell University Press, Ithaca, New York, pp. 224-27.
15. Quoted in Kisan World, Dec. 1987, p. 39.
16. Quoted in A.J. Coale and E.M. Hoover — Population Growth and Economic Development in Low Income Countries, Princeton 1958, p. 121.
17. Bhanu Pratap Singh, — Do Farmers Get a Fair Deal?, The Hindu Survey of Agriculture , 1988-89, p. 17.
18. *Ibid.*
19. Quoted in — Bhanu Pratap Singh, *opt. cit.*
20. R.P. Singh — Challenge of Dry Farming. The Hindu Survey of Agriculture, 1988, p. 56.
21. Bhanu Pratap Singh — Do Farmers Get a Fair Deal?, The Hindu Survey of Agriculture, 1988, p. 17.
22. M.S. Swaminathan — Time for New Orientation. The Hindu Survey of Agriculture, 1988, p. 7.
23. *Ibid.,* p. 7.
24. T.P. Ojha, Need for a Long-Term Policy the Hindu Survey of Agriculture, 1988, pp. 151, 152.
25. Randhawa, N.S. — Accent on Nutrient Management, The Hindu Survey of Agriculture, 1988, p. 157.
26. S. Jayraj — Integrated Approach Vital, The Hindu Survey of Agriculture, 1988, p. 165.
27. *Ibid.,* p. 165.
28. Bhanu Pratap Singh, *op. cit.,* p. 19.
29. A.D.R. Vol. 5, No. 1 — Commodity Price and Fertilizer News, referred by Bhanu Pratap Singh, *opt. cit.,* p. 19.

2
Critical Review of Agricultural Finance

2.1. Role of Credit in Agriculture

Credit, no doubt to any sector is an additional oxygen to breath better for better health of the economy. Any lendable finance *i.e.* credit dare to invest for profit earnings, and lender come forward to lend for such activities, because they have surety of returning the lent money. So, initially trade, commerce and industrial activities had the major attractions of credit Many industrialists were established their banks for self-development during the beginning of 20th century. Agriculture though a core sector, was not practised in a business line; because of its subsistence nature during old days. However, the situation now-a-days is changing, particularly since the installation of green revolution movement Before the nationalisation of major commercial banks, no institutional credit was provided for agriculture sector except by co-operatives and Govt. But today about 633 per cent of debt belongs to institutional credit agencies, which was only 123 per cent during 1951-52. However, even to-day the share of non-institutional credit agencies is not negligible (37%).

Credit to agriculture is an essential input for farm development Agricultural development can be contributed through various essential factors. A.T. Mosher[1] identifies five essentials of agricultural development, they are: (i) market for farm product, (ii) constantly changing technology, (iii) local availability of supplies and equipment, (iv) production incentives, (v) transportation. He also suggests[2], five accelerators for agricultural development, *viz.* (a) education for production, (b) production credit, (c) group action by farmers, (d) improving and expanding agricultural land, (e) national planning for agricultural development. Production credit is one of the essentials for agricultural development. Agricultural credit will help in extending the existing areas of cultivable land under crops and help in making structural changes in relation to the available area of cultivable land. The common goal of credit is higher production; where higher production is not intended only for higher consumption purposes is supposed to be a source of funds for investment *i.e.* capital stock. The vicious circle of low productivity will be broken through creating this kind of capital stock. In determining the nature of capital for agriculture, Bringer G.K.[3] includes not only the capital items in the balance sheet of agriculture but takes into consideration capital embodied in community facilities (such as schools, roads and dams) market facilities, technology and certain activities subserving the production. First, it is essential to take into consideration the current loans and similarly make an allowance for non-balance sheet items of a capital nature mentioned above. Credit for agriculture is required for efficient farm functioning because of following reasons:

(i) meagre resources of poor farmers whose number is very large,

(ii) purchase of major agricultural inputs outside the farm,

(ii) backwardness of farmers,

(iii) lengthy production period causing higher credit needs, and

(iv) widespread rural indebtedness.[4] Indian agriculturalists experience these difficulties. Agricultural credit is required to improve agricultural practices and purchase of input for growing yield. The role of agricultural credit in agricultural development is better explained by R.D. Sharma[5] in the following manner:

> "It consists in enlarging the net cultivable area by bringing waste and fallow land under cultivation, providing manure and chemical fertilizers, protection of land, the provision of irrigation, making large amounts of fixed and working capital available to agriculture, changing farm organisation, enlarging its share of gross national product and increasing labour return in agriculture. It has also some bearing on the problem of ensuring fair returns to agriculture. Adequate and timely finance enhance the withholding capacity of the cultivators and their bargaining position with the increase

in the holding capacity of the cultivators, the huge post-harvest market glut may be avoided which is the major factor in lowering the agricultural prices just after the harvest.... Right type of credit penetrates into agriculture and injects an element of healthy competition and concrete commercial calculations in farm operations. It turns agriculture into 'a way of living' as distinct from 'a way of life'. The subsistence farming gives way to commercial farming, the simply process of production makes room for mechanised operations and the attitudinal changes sweep the length and breadth of the countryside. Once the match-stick of credit ignites the flame, better managerial skills sustain it and a holy process of one inducing the other and covering all comes into effect. Thus the role of credit consists in laying the foundation stone of farm revolution and maintaining the structure built upon it."

Agricultural credit thus results into the commercialisation of agriculture instead of subsistence farming. The Indian experience has shown this attitudinal performance: as and when agricultural credit is taken either from Govt. or financial institutions, the agriculture has changed into commercial purpose, mainly because of the compelling need for amortizing the loans taken. Moreover, it is profitable because both farmers and credit agencies gain. Agriculture requires credit for the purpose of capital formation on land and current expenditure on farm, non-farm business expenditure, and other expenditures etc. Credit is needed for capital, current, family and other expenses. But only the provision of credit to agriculture will not solve the problem. The big-push with comprehensive socio-economic and socio-cultural efforts are essential. We can improve the economic efficiency by providing various inputs reasonably among which credit is the most important. However, this should not become full time work of Government. Credit is a bad master if it is mismanaged. It is like the French proverb, "credit supports the farmer as the hangman's rope supports the hanged. However, if it is used in proper and efficient manner "it can serve as an elevator".

The main purpose of credit borrowing is related to the economic development of a country in general, and the development of borrower in particular. Credit in banking is the actual or prospective debtors' power or ability to obtain temporary money or goods or services in exchange by offering his promise of future payment with interest. It is the man's confidence expressed in another man which may bring economic and social change in rural areas.

2.1.1. *Economic Role*

(a) A vast majority of our farms are very small in size. Out of 90 million, more than 80 million operational farms holding in the country are below 2 hectares in size. All such farmers are incapable to get even a daily bread from their size of holding. If, however, they are provided a credit either for their farm or for their subsidiary activities, they can improve their standard of living. Credit to such farmers should have a special character, because; (i) agriculture is a complex industry, (ii) a considerable proportion of them have no assets neither sufficient land, nor any asset, (iii) moreover land is a shrinkage resource to them, and (iv) difficult to forecast risks and uncertainties. This credit cannot be on the lines of industrial, trade and commercial credit. This should be so because the fate of our economy is dependent on such small and marginal farmers.

(b) A majority of younger generation of rural India is reluctant to practice agriculture. But as the future of our agriculture depends on them, so, credit should attract and retain youth in farming and allied rural occupations. If they look towards agriculture on a business line, they can be provided with credit which will make them remain and develop in the same sector.

(c) Investment in farm activities brings employment opportunities to the unemployed both in industrial and agriculture sectors. For example sugarcane crop generates additional employment for 35 man-days per year, per hectare area of cultivation.

(d) Production credit improves the crop yield and increase the income level This will bring in the multiplier and acceleration effects on consumption, investment, income, saving, employment in agriculture, industry and service sectors of the economy. A.S. Kahlon[6] remarks, "In a subsistence agriculture most of the farm inputs will be raised on the farm but as agriculture moves on the road to progressive modernisation, the proportion of purchased inputs will tend to rise, and most of the technological inputs such as fertilizer, pesticides, mechanical input and particularly power in an energy intensive modern agriculture have to come from other sectors of the economy. Again significant increases in the agricultural productivity would come through investment in irrigation and compel monetary infrastructure."

(e) Credit motivates a farmer to cultivate cash crop for amortizing the borrowed credit. And cash crops help to develop agro-industries.

(f) The wastes or unutilised resources can possibly be mobilised for further economic development through credit facility.

(g) The modernisation of agriculture is possible through provision of credit facilities. Agricultural sector can be brought in a business sector with the help of credit, where a farmer can think of cost and benefit of his farm undertakings.

(h) Agricultural capital is less mobile, and a farmer finds it difficult to divert his resources and shift from the cultivation of a particular set of crops to another set because of the presence of factors such as weather, suitability of soil and climate etc. That is why subsidiary activities can be developed through adding further credit to the capital for example poultry, dairy, horticulture, sericulture etc.

(i) As our farmers are indebted by non-institutional credit agencies to some extent, credit facilities from institutional agencies are essential. Dr. S.C. Mehta has commented that, if credit is to make a significant impact on agriculture, it is essential that credit machinery be expanded much more rapidly than would be feasible through non-institutional means alone. Institutional channels of credit may play a complimentary or a substitute role *vis-a-vis* the traditional channels.[7]

2.1.2. Social Role

A formulation of economic development policy must not ignore the social and cultural factors, which are more specifically the grit and highly enterprising spirit of peasantry of the state, and to which renowned personalities have paid growing tributes. Credit is indeed a force and property of socio-cultural change which is rather internally hidden in the society. This is so because:

(a) normally rural women are economical and work more than men and contribute more to development. David Mac Clelland adds that due to the subordination of women in the developing countries, it is men rather than women who are often exposed to achievement oriented value outside the domestic scene.[8] They may better utilise the credit, borrowed so far. Some economic activities, which really uplift the rural women to self-reliance by providing loans for milk- animal, sericulture, apiculture, aquaculture and other cottage and small industrial activities. So credit may be a incentive to bring out the women from traditional subordination.

(b) a few decades ago, our farmers were used to borrow loans from money-lenders to celebrate marriage, birth and other cultural activities etc. Even today, to some extent farmers borrow for the same purpose, under the guise of production credit and use it for other unproductive purposes;

(c) indebtedness makes a borrower to work hard and produce more. In an underdeveloped country like ours hard work is more necessary for production at increasing rates. The whole family integrate to work hard to repay the loans borrowed;

(d) social structure may undergo structural change, and the traditions may get rugged;

(e) the credit given, shall educate, discipline and guide the borrower. It may be granted only to those who think to plan and to save. Moreover, it brings mutual help and self-help.

Thus the quantitative states of society may be raised and maintained with the help of credit.

2.1.3. Technological Role

Technological role means application of modern technical know-how to the different phases of production through borrowed capital. Credit may be used for current expenses and investment in agriculture current expenses include, (a) the expenditure on bio-chemical technology, (b) tillage and preparation of land, (c) labour charges, (d) seedling and plantation and harvesting expenses, etc. And investment in agriculture includes: (a) on-farm investment like systematic land development, minor irrigation, soil conservation etc., (b) farm-mechanisation investments in power sprayers, winnowers, threshers, power tillers, tractors harvester combines etc., (c) diversified purposive investments in horticulture, sericulture, apiculture (bee-keeping), pisciculture (in land and marine fisheries), aquaculture, dairy, poultry, sheep and goat rearing, piggery etc., and (d) investment in marketing and storages, which include storage go downs, market yards, silos etc. The modern bio-chemical and mechanical technology is possible only when credit hypothecation facility is available to farmers.

Investment in land assets is only possible if there is a profit margin (that is more than rate of interest to be paid to lending agencies). Recent investments are mostly hypothecated by lending agencies. Recently developed leasing companies, co-operatives should come forward to improve technological developments in agriculture sector.

As discussed above, credit is one of the essentials for increasing agricultural production. History has proved with ample evidence that the persons engaged in agricultural business cannot carry on their business without outside finance. Agricultural credit is a problem when it cannot be obtained. It is also a problem when it can be had but in such a form that on the whole it does more harm than good. In India it is this two-fold problem of inadequacy and unsuitability that is perennially presented by agricultural credit[9] Memoria and Saksena have given the following as the special characteristics of agricultural finance:[10]

1. The agriculturists' need for finance is generally constant and is not affected quickly and substantially by changes in output.
2. The agriculturists undertake a process of production prospects which are difficult to anticipate and more difficult to control.
3. The asset of the agriculturists is land, which is not suitable as security for loans at least in the framework of commercial banking.
4. The agriculturists must carry the entire risk of his productive operation himself because unlike industry, he cannot transfer a part of his prospective profits by inducing his lenders to share in his risks.
5. The persistent small scale organisation of agriculture limits available credit to the owner and prevents resource to raising capital by device of forming a limited liability company and financing by share floatation.
6. Agricultural finance has peculiar problems which require special treatment, because of small units of production to be managed without control over the yield and quality.
7. Credit is more necessary in agriculture because it takes months to receive the return of its labour and the supply of agricultural produce is seasonal while the demand exists all the year round which makes financial arrangements much more unavoidable in order to make adjustments of both and stabilise prices.

Thus an importance of farm finance has been established very aptly by the following lines:

> "Only that village is fit to live, in which there is a money-lender to lend at need, Vaidya to treat in illness, a Brahmin to administer the soul and a stream that does not dry up in summers."[11]

2.2. Agricultural Finance in India

Agricultural credit may be defined as the amount of investible funds made available for farm business, and farmer's family needs. In the past, agricultural credit was confined to a few needy farmers and a few elite lenders. During the drought conditions and scanty rainfalls, farmers used to get food grains from rich farmers (*i.e.* who have a surplus food grains all the time) on the condition that the same would be returned with interest after harvesting the next crop in the form of additional quantity of borrowed food grains. This was known as "Wadi" system in southern Maharashtra region.[12]

The people engaged in such activities were village traders and feudal lords, who gradually moved towards the full-fledged job of money lending and were then called as money-lenders, who still hold their position in rural area. Security for the loans were precious ornaments and durable copper utensils etc. for smaller amount of loans. If the amount was high, then farmers used to lease their land to the lender. There were two types of land leasing: (i) the ownership of whole land area to be retained by the lender until a borrower refund the borrowed amount. A lender manages to cultivate the leased land, and the whole yield went to the lender, (ii) in other form, a land area was leased for specific period *i.e.* 3,5,7,10 years, according to amount. The cultivation and yield remained with the lender for the said period. After completion of the period, the land was returned to the original owner (borrower). This practice still prevails in South Maharashtra and North Karnataka regions. The cause and purpose of borrowing generally, relates to either drought or failure of crops or extravagant spending on cultural activities. The amount of debit differs according to various sections of peasantry. R.P. Rana[13] has proved this position with various references. He classified various sections of peasantry into three groups. First, there were the low caste, landless rural poor fulfilled the labour needs of the entire land owning peasantry. Through the operation of the caste system, the landless were restrained, from acquiring land for self-cultivation.[14] Secondly, there were the small-scale dependent producers, who sold, part of their labour and/or rented in drought animals and a significant amount of other agricultural equipment. These peripatetic cultivators were known as Pahis.[15] Thirdly, there were those petty producers who were more or less self-sufficient in as much as they did not hire out or hire in labour and who just about lived at the subsistence level, though occasionally they contracted loans for purchasing agricultural equipments.[16] Other than these sections, there was a class of money-lenders who supplied credit to needy farmers. The rise and spread of this class seem to have a universal historical background.[17] According to the above classification the third class occasionally borrowed. Credit was not required all the time. In certain unavoidable circumstances farmers used to borrow on the basis of personal credit in the village. The natural calamities like failure of rainfall, drought, famines etc. were the causes of borrowing. In times of climatic adversity almost all the three classes referred to above required credit.

Even Deccan Riots Report[18] has pointed out that the irregularity of the monsoon in the Deccan, the consequent precarious nature of cultivation in the area, and also supposed improvidence and 'extravagance' of the rayat especially at such times as weddings are causes for agricultural indebtedness. In Bombay, intensive surveys revealed that the burden of average debt per family varied from ₹ 115 in the Konkan, to ₹ 225 in the transition tract and ₹ 500 in the cotton growing zone.[19] In Bombay the estimate of families free from debt was 13 per cent in Sind, 23 per cent in South Gujarat, 21 per cent in North Gujarat and 29 per cent in the Konkan.[20] Some quantitative estimates of rural indebtedness in Madras province in 1946 are, available in Naidu's[21] report in which the causes of rural indebtedness were classified as (a) basic, and (b) alternative. Basic reasons include the nature of the economy like weather, soil conditions, and the size of land holdings. The alternative reasons include factors like low price, very high rate of interest, natural growth of population, litigation etc.

At the end of the 19th century, the problem of indebtedness had become a serious problem. Due to high rate of interest and other exploitations, farmers mooted to discontented against money-lenders. The policies implemented by the Govt. to face the drought, minimised the pressure of revolt. During the period even policy so far recommended and implemented for sound and effective agricultural credit system was the result of either because of the drought condition or rioting against money-lenders. In order to meet the drought situation, the states (Northern States of 17th and 18th centuries) ordered the advancing of takkavi loans at the rate of ₹ 2 per bigha[22] to the peasants.[23] In some places puttag[24] concessions in land revenue were also granted. But the first outcome of the rioting against moneylenders appears to have taken place in Supa in May 1875, a village about forty miles from Poona.[25]

As early as 1882, Sir Willium Wedderburn and Justice Ranade prepared a scheme for establishing the agricultural banks to provide loans to farmers. Their scheme was not accepted in the form in which it was prepared, but its essential features were embodied in the Land Improvement and Agriculturists' Loans Acts (XIX of 1883 and XII of 1884 respectively) under which the agriculturists could borrow from the Government for productive purposes at about 6 per cent.[26] Thus the 'puttag' concession, the Deccan Agriculturists Relief Acts, 1875 and 1891-92 and the concept of agricultural bank are the outcome of either natural causes or unsatisfactory credit system of early India. In 1892, Fredrick Nicholson was appointed by Madras Govt. to report on the advisability of starting agricultural and land banks in the presidency. The Famine Commission's report, with great struggle and efforts led to the conception of the Bill of 1901, which was later enacted into Co-operative Credit Societies Act of 25th March 1904. The principal feature of the Bill was to minimise cultivators who had been unable to pay the assessment during the last year owing to sheer inability to that of daily labourers or tenants at will.[27] The 1904 Act emphasised credit through co-operative principles. Various Acts (1912, 1914, 1919 and the Provincial Acts) followed, and after Independence, co-operation is given a unique place in Five Year Plan outlays. Naturally co-operative movement flourished not only in respect of credit but in other areas like, marketing processing, farming, housing industry, dairy, labour and other non-credit cooperatives etc. But the initial thrust of the movement was to satisfy the credit hunger of farmers. Meanwhile a movement was also initiated upliftment of the poorest of the poor. But today apart from agricultural credit societies the movement is spreading in other sectors. So, sectoral and the regional imbalances are observed in co-operative movement.

Since the installation of co-operative movement, co-operative credit societies and Govt. were the only institutional source of borrowing meant for agricultural development. But most of them were wrecked by the opposition of the money-lenders. Therefore, the growth of co-operatives is observed in members instead of quality (See Table 2.1). Though the member of co-operatives stood high, the share of co-operatives credit is declining,

	Years between		No. of Societies	No. of Members	Amount of Working capital
1.	1906-07 to 1916-17	10 Years	39.4	7.7	2.9
2.	1916-17 to 1927-28	11 Years	13.7	0.3	8.5
3.	1927-28 to 1938-39	11 Years	2.2	5.2	3.0
4.	1938-39 to 1945-46	7 Years	5.1	7.9	6.4

Table No. 2.1: Growth Rates of Co-operative Credit Societies

Table 2.2 reveals the fact of Bombay Presidency that during the inception of co-operative movement a share of crop finance lent by co-operatives was high during the period between 1946 to 1949 excepting the loans in kind.

Years	Amount advanced through agencies of		
	Co-operative Societies	Revenue Department	Money Lenders
Up to 30-6-1946	5,61,553 (82.42)	1,18,080 + 6 Khandis 8 Moundis in kind	1640
1946-47	23,39,609 (87.47)	3,33,060	2058
1947-48	51,77,507 (92.21)	4,28,060 + 257 Khandis 3 Mounds and 14 Payees in kind	9166
1948-49	78,30,994 (99.78)	7,890 + 440 Mounds in kind	9370

Table No. 2.2: Crop Finance

Source: The Co-operative Movement in Bombay State—K.N. Naik, 1953, p. 34.

Notes: 1. The data in parenthesis indicate the per cent to total except kind loans,
2. 1 Khandi = 12 bags or 20 Mounds.
1 Mound = 40 Kg.
1 Payee = 4 sheer
1 Sheer = approx 800 grams.

During the period, the share of co-operatives goes on increasing. The tendency to borrow from co-operative increased during the period. The debt issued by money-lenders has increased nine times, while the credit issued by co-operatives increased by about sixteen fold during the period between 1946-49. This continue till the nationalisation of major commercial banks.

After nationalisation, commercial banks came forward to lend for priority sector including agriculture. During the period after nationalisation the share of co-operatives in total refinance disbursement fell down from 96.52 per cent in 1969 to 44.19 per cent in 1985.[28] However, the share of Maharashtra and Andhra Pradesh stood higher (63%) than other states in this respect.

Agencies	AIRCS 1951	AIRDIS 1961	NCAER 1971	NSS 37th round
1. Government	3.3	2.3	3.6	4.5
2. Co-operation	3.1	15.5	22.7	28.7
3. Comm. Banks	0.9	0.6	4.0	28.0
4. Money-lenders, traders, commission agents	75.0	58.0	49.6	20.2
5. Friends and Relatives	14.2	8.8	18.8	18.6
6. Landlords and others	3.3	14.5	1.3	
Total	100.0	100.0	100.0	100.0

Table No. 2.3: Proportion of Agricultural Borrowings from Different Agencies According to Various Surveys (in %)

In 1951 All India Rural Credit Survey Committee was appointed. According to this Committee the share of co-operative in total agricultural borrowings was 3.1 per cent, which increased to 15.5 per cent in 1961. And in 1971 the share of co-operative was 22.7 per cent. In 1981 the percentage was 28.7 (see Table 2.3). The share of commercial banks and co-operatives is almost the same. Indeed they are competing with each other. The share of commercial banks is observed to increase only after nationalistion. At the end of Dec. 1950 the advances of scheduled commercial banks were only 2.3 per cent, which raised to 16.6 per cent at the end of Dec. 1982. (See Table 2.4). Their share in respect of trade has decreased from 31.7 per cent to 18.7 per cent, but the sub-total of trade and industry increased from 63.8 per cent to 73.9 per cent during the same period.

		End of Dec. 1950	Last Friday Dec. 1982
1.	Agriculture (including plantation)	2.3	16.6
2.	Industry	32.1	55.2
3.	Trade	31.7	18.7
	Sub-total of industry and trade	63.8	100.0
4.	Others	33.9	9.1
	Total	100.0	100.0

Table No. 2.4: Pattern of Advances of Scheduled Commercial Banks

(in percentages)

Source: Centre for Monitoring Indian Economy: Basic Statistics, All India, August, 1986.

Table No. 2.5 illustrates Public Sector Banks Advances to Priority Sectors.

It reveals that the number of accounts advances to priority sector increased by about hundred times between 1969 to 1985. About 84.32 per cent of advances are direct loans in Dec. 1985. Thus the growth of advances to agriculture is observed after independence.

The share of co-operatives in 1972-73 was 82.89 per cent, which fell to 51.14 per cent in 1984-85. While the share of scheduled commercial banks has increased from 1.80 per cent to 39.90 per cent during the same period (See Table 2.6). Agricultural credit is indispensable to agriculture, it is equally essential that it should be cheap, safe. It is one of the dudes of the state, especially of an agricultural country to ensure that agricultural credit is fully institutionalised and insulated against all kinds of risks arising out of natural hazards and from misuse/abuse by the borrowers.

Sectors	No. of Accounts (000)			Amount Outstanding (₹ Crores)		
	June 1969	Dec. 1985	Dec. 1986	June 1969	Dec. 1985	Dec. 1986
1. Agriculture	165	16000	16858	162	8793	10138
(i) Direct	160	15027	15964	40	7415	8876
(ii) Indirect	5	973	894	122	1378	1262
2. Small-Scale Sector*	53	2188	NA	257	9354	NA
(i) Road, water trans. operations	2	592	NA	6	1883	NA
(ii) S.S. Industries	51	1595	NA	251	7396	NA
(iii) Setting up of industrial estates	-	1	NA	-	75	NA
3. Other Priority Sector	42	5680	NA	22	2416	NA
(i) Retail trade and small business	33	3989	NA	19	1721	NA
(ii) Professional self employ. persons	8	1613	NA	2	653	NA
(iii) Education	1	66	NA	1	33	NA
(iv) Indirect finances to priority sector others (lending to SC/ST) corporations/ organizations	-	5	NA	-	5	NA
4. Housing loans to SC/ ST and weaker sections	-	164	NA	-	64	NA
5. Consumption loans**	-	162	NA	-	21	NA
Total priority sector	260	24194	26157	441	20648	23811
6. Exports	-	-	-	204	48067	54642
(i) Total bank credit	-	-	-	3016	-	-
(ii) % to priority sector advance to total bank credit	-	-	-	14.6	42.9	43,6

Table No. 2.5: Public Sector Banks Advances to Priority Sectors (As on the last Friday)

*Relate to number of units (a) Data provisional - Nil

**Data available from Dec. 1981 only, NA — Not available.

Note: Data for 1969 are from Banking Statistics, GoI and for subsequent years from Rural Planning and Credit Deptt. RBI, Currency and Finance Report, 1986-87, p. 169.

Loans issued during	Co-op	State Govts.	Scheduled Comm. Banks	RRBs	Total
1972-73	957.9	176.8	20.9	-	1155.6
	(82.89)	(15.29)	(1.80)	-	(100.0)
1973-74	8767(R)	90.8	219.2	-	9097(R)
	(96.58)	(1.00)	(2.41)		
1974-75	1040.0(R)	77.5	27.43	-	1391.8(R)
	(74.72)	(5.56)	(19.70)		
1975-76	1186.7(R)	81.5	404.9	1.5	1674.6(R)
	(70.86)	(4.86)	(24.17)	(0.08)	
1976-77	1366.6(R)	85.5	565.0(E)	11.6(E)	2028.7(E)
	(67.36)	(4.21)	(27.85)	(0.57)	
1982-83	2717	188	1225	222	4352
	(62.43)	(4.31)	(28.14)	(5.10)	
1983-84	2938	185	1825	263	5211
	(56.38)	(3.55)	(35.02)	(5.04)	
1984-85	3154(RE)	241	2461	310	6166
	(51.15)	(3.90)	(39.91)	(5.22)	
1985-86	3755(E)	354	NA	402(P)	NA
1986-87	4273	488(RE)	NA	NA	NA
	(-)	(-)	(-)	(-)	(-)

Table No. 2.6: Direct Institutional Finance for Agriculture and Allied Activities

(₹ Crores)

The data in parenthesis indicate the % to total
R = Revised, RE = Revised Estimates
P = Provisional, NA = Not Available.

That is why our institutional loans to agriculture *i.e.* cultivators increased from 18.4 per cent in 1961 to 63.2 per cent in 1981. But the non- institutional loans to non-cultivators are higher than institutional. The share of non-institutional loans to non-cultivators decreased only by 26.2 per cent between 1961 to 1981. (See Table 2.7). Even today we must not ignore the role of non-institutional agencies. Any way credit is elevator to serve the agriculture and agriculturists.

		Institutional	Non-Institutional	All Agencies
Cultivators	1961	18.4	81.6	100.0
	1971	31.7	63.3	100.0
	1981	63.2	36.8	100.0
Non-Cultivators	1961	10.5	89.5	100.0
	1971	10.8	89.2	100.0
	1981	36.7	63.3	100.0
All Types	1961	17.3	82.7	100.0
	1971	29.2	70.9	100.0
	1981	612	38.8	100.0

Table No. 2.7: % of Cash Debt from Institutional and Non-institutional Credit Agencies to Total Outstanding

Source: NSS 37th Round, p. 17.

Mr. Nicholson observed that, "credit is a weapon that may destroy the unskillful wielder, it is helpful or destructive according as it is used or abused." That is why, investment in human factor is always emphasised, in almost all policies and strategies. Instead of short term materialistic brightness of development, watchful development strategies should have to be adopted. Otherwise a short-run development may move us towards decay.

2.3. Classification of Agricultural Finance

As seen earlier, both institutional and non-institutional credit agencies come forward to issue agricultural loans. Most of the role is played by co-operative agencies, indeed their emergence was meant for the agricultural purpose. But the major flow was harnessed by rich farmers. Prof. Raj Krishna estimated that only 1/3 of the total flow of rural credit provided by banks and co-operatives has gone to small farmer households even though they constitute nearly 2/3 of all agricultural households.[29] Even today the loan amount disbursed to weaker section by banks is about less than one per cent.[30] The tension remained the same, in connection with agricultural finance though we have multi-agency approach in banking sector. Government has been adopting dualistic policies in respect of involvement of commercial banks and co-operatives in agricultural co-operatives, and in effect commercial banks are competing in issuing credit to agricultural sector. The entry of the commercial banks in the field of agricultural financing created more problems than it was expected to solve.[31] But the idea behind the entry of commercial banks in agricultural finance was to solve the Himalayan problem of agricultural backwardness.

The network of financial institutions in India may be categorised into two: (a) Unorganised (non-institutional) and (b) organised (institutional), both of which are mainly related to money market. Capital market is not related to the problems of agriculture. However, indirectly they come to the rescue of agriculture through money markets *via* central banks.

Agricultural credit may be direct or indirect. Direct credit is for the cultivators' farming operations and acquisition of assets. Indirect credit is for developing agricultural infrastructure like inputs distribution and co-operative marketing and processing units. This type of credit also includes the credit to small farmers, landless labourers and other credit agencies, artisan etc. Institutional (organised) and non-institutional (unorganised) agencies issue both direct and indirect credits to agriculture. One step further, non-institutional agencies supply credit even to cultural activities of borrowers.

Agricultural finance may be categorised into purpose or causes, because it is made available for various purposes. For example, agriculture, pisciculture, apiculture, sericulture, land development, farm mechanisation, drought animals, milk animals, forest development, piggery, poultry, plantations, bio-gas, gobar gas, market-yard, dairy, service centres, go downs, cold storages, etc. Various credit agencies come forward to lend for these allied activities. Agricultural finance may be classified according to agro-business for which credit is essential. This may be hypothecation loans to farm business items. And other loans like cash credits are issued on economic status of the borrowers. Production credit is another way of borrowing which may be classified into settlement, development and equipment credit to agriculture.

Agricultural credit may be secured or unsecured. Secured loans may be real or mortgage credit, chattel and collateral credit and personal credit based on three corresponding divisions of capital *viz.* land, goods and character. Unsecured credits are mainly issued to such borrowers who are members of urban banks and urban co-operative societies etc. Other than these co-operative banks and societies no credit agency dare to issue unsecured loans. Friends and relatives are another source of borrowings, from where, unsecured loans can be available.

Credit may be generally classified according to the length of credit *i.e.* short-term credit, medium term credit and long-term credit. Short-term credit (up to 15 months) is available for current expenses of agriculture *e.g.*, crop production and purchase of inputs etc. Medium term credit (up to 2 to 5 years) is available for the purpose of land development, minor irrigation, farm machinery, implements, milk animal and other smaller capital value assets, etc. And long-term credit (between 5 to 25 years) is available for long-term capital assets in agriculture. For example, plantation, integrated development of agriculture and allied activities, and live stocks etc. Certain agencies are only meant for long-term investment in agriculture; for example District Co-operative Agricultural and Rural Development Banks issue only long-term credit. And Primary Agricultural Co-operative Societies issue only short and medium term loans for agricultural purposes. Commercial banks can issue ST & MT credits classified according to the period. Even large size multipurpose societies can supply long-term credit for agriculture. The proportion of farmers who borrow short-term loans is higher than those who borrow medium and long-term credits, and the proportion of medium term borrowings is higher than long-term credit. It means our farmers still need to borrow for current expenses; they do not dare to invest in medium and long-term investment assets, but developed agriculture which is normally irrigated, needs medium and long-term credits.

Generally agricultural borrowers are agriculturists, individual owner cultivators, tenants, sharecroppers, registered and unregistered partnership farms, companies, estates, co-operative societies and public sector corporations etc., who borrow according to their economies from where the credit or loan facilities are available. So, a borrower is free to choose a credit agency, which is relevant to his purpose and the choice depends upon his agro-business and economic status and repayment capacity. But after the recent establishment of NABARD, we have been to move towards a special hierarchy for agricultural and rural development credit. But no specialisation is observed as yet. However, one can accept and expect the role of co-operatives in agricultural finance, and they have specialised in supplying credit to agriculture and allied activities; but they face various bottlenecks and constraints. Therefore, a special hierarchy is suggested from NABARD to co-operative village Bank.

2.4. Significance of Co-operative Credit

As seen in the earlier chapter, both agriculture and rural development are vital for the health of our economy. It is also essential for the survival of democratic framework and socialistic pattern of society. But in case of agricultural finance no justification is given. The urban area has varieties of financial institutions located for the benefit of urban population. For example, public sector, scheduled, non-scheduled urban banks, urban co-operative credit societies and the like are located in urban area. For every 7371 urban[31], 5893 metropolitan and 11,104 semi-urban people there is a commercial bank. While about 31,429 people have one commercial bank in rural area during April-December 1988, Industrial sector has broadly well-served by many financial institutions like IDBI, IFCs, ICICI, NIDC etc. and growing network of commercial banks. But the hinterland rural area appears to be ill-served in credit facilities, where agriculture, a core sector is located. Only co-operative, to some extent, is providing credit facilities to rural sector. Although, there are some impressive specialised credit institutions set up for agriculture purpose, RBI, Public Sector Banks, AFC, ARDC, LDB, RRB, NCDC etc., they face varieties of limitations, they cannot be held responsible to fulfil the rural credit need. "NABARD started with high hopes and fanfare and 'has no doubt grown in staff strength—a phenomenon common to most public sector institutions, but whether this growth has been matched by increased efficiency, is a moot question."[32] Credit, either urban or rural, is a means to develop our major sectors, but it only caters to credit-worthy borrowers and people who have some income. Displaying net profit in their balance sheets need not be the sole aim of public credit institutions. Social compulsions of uplifting the rural poor specially the landless labour and the freed bonded labour who have no collateral to offer — except their freedom, should not be lost sight of."[33] Such people are in need of credit and can secure betterment of their life through that. But credit agency should dare to lend to such section of rural area and backward area. Co-operatives is the only sector providing helping-hand to such down-trodden masses both from urban and rural area. Co-operative urban banks and societies have already played a significant role in urban development. This is the situation in rural area through co-operative societies linked vertically and horizontally.

Co-operation in India started with agricultural credit and even today agricultural credit dominates the spectrum of co-operative activity in the country. There is a fascinating interlinking of co-operative enterprises encompassing social, educational, medical, cultural, economic and political components of the society. The peoples' needs are better understood and stratified through co-operative planning. Effective co-operatives, tend to reduce the need for state action and lighten the load carried by Government. Various government actions require intermediatory agencies like co-operatives, voluntary agencies and semi-government agencies. Under-developed regions may be developed specially through such agencies, because they already have self-disciplined strategies to solve the socio-economic needs of the society. Government recognises co-operatives as the agent for carrying out certain functions such as procurement of food grains and distribution of agricultural requisites. Govt. gives preferential treatment to co-operatives in marketing construction and gives them some fiscal concessions.

The significance of any kind of enterprise may be judged by asking the following questions:

(a) Has the agency the ability to provide institutional framework, which is capable of bringing forth positive efforts to enhance the peoples' living standards, and expand the involvement in social needs?
(b) Is the agency able to raise sufficient internal as well as external funds? Does the agency have trained staff and training programme for members?

(c) Does the agency help to develop the social and economic structure and engage in research activity in various fields and sectors of the economy?

(d) Is the agency viable, self-governed and self-sufficient? Co-operatives satisfy many of these conditions to a large extent. Moreover, it is a sector, which is more appropriate in a mixed economy like India.

"Co-operation as a form of organisation emerged in the capitalist economies, when conditions of perfect competition failed to work in these countries. Co-operation works successfully when conditions of monopoly and imperfections in the market economy tend to dominate. It may not emerge when competition is working all right, when private ownership is the most accepted system for organising its economic activities.[34] Co-operation is a remedy for the harmful effects of private and capitalistic enterprises. And, therefore, F. Hall and WJP, Watking quoted, Dr. King, "The Great beauty of co-operation is that it may begin without any capital at all."[35]

Co-operative sector, thus, plays a vital role in agricultural and rural development in India, especially co-operative credit has given the content of quality to the movement. Agricultural growth may take place through incentives of credit and co-operative credit movement can flourish only if agriculture prospers. The experience of Egypt, Mexico and other countries reveals that redistribution of land if accompanied by a measure for strengthening co-operatives providing credit and supplying technical assistance, is more likely to raise, than to decrease agricultural production.[36] The report of the Committee on Integration of Co-operative Credit Institutions (Hazari, 1976) expresses confidence that the co-operative credit system can fully play its expected role in agricultural development if the imbalances in its growth are corrected and if it is enabled to provide credit facilities in an integrated manner. Commercial banks rush towards developed regions, and there will be a competition among co-operatives and commercial credit institutions. Such competition is nothing but a "Competition between two sectors". Co-operatives have tendency to rush towards underdeveloped regions. Kamath Committee has rightly pointed out that the multi-agency approach has given birth to a manner of problems, *i.e.* danger like overfinancing, underfinancing and multi-financing leading to financial indiscipline and diversion of scarce resources for unproductive purposes. There are also some problems of overlapping and duplication of banking facilities and consequent wasteful expenditure, besides unhealthy competition.[37] Generally co-operation and particularly co-operative credit has brought new hopes among the weaker sections of the society. Pandit Jawaharlal Nehru[38] considered the test of the movement's success on how far it helps and brings benefits to the socially and economically weaker sections of organisations/community. Co-operative form of organisation has today assumed a place of pride as a distinct economic system. Moreover, co-operative credit is cheaper than other credit agencies. All principles of agricultural credit are tested well in the co-operative credit agencies: (a) credit is cheap and safe, (b) has an effective linkage for recoveries, (c) is available also for consumption purposes, (d) issue all types of credit *(i.e.,* short-term, medium-term and long-term, (e) has linkages between various types of co-operatives, (f) is disbursed only after examining the need.

Mohinder Singh[39] highlighted co-operative credit as an instrument of agricultural growth on the basis of following points:

1. An essential condition to produce an atmosphere of dynamic credit is that technique for improving productivity should have been developed and convincingly demonstrated to the farmers. In other words, there should be a well-developed extension service, supported adequately by research stations, and working closely with the co-operative organisation to create among the farmers; a demand for improved agricultural requisites and implements.
2. The co-operatives should be able to provide adequate and timely credit to cover the production as well as essential need for consumption on the basis of the repaying capacity of the farmer. It is equally important that the co-operatives should be able to recover loans satisfactorily, if possible through sale proceeds of crops, which constitute the main means of repayment, and they should cover as large a proportion of the farm population as possible.

3. Multi-purpose co-operatives combining credit, supply and marketing offer a possibility of dealing with these problems in an integrated way. An alternative though somewhat less attractive, in the light of the hitherto limited experience is to have several single purpose societies dealing with credit, marketing and supply, and working in close co-ordination. In some cases, this approach may raise the problem of making three primary societies viable instead of one. And, moreover, the availability of personnel with requisite experience is limited.
4. It is important, however, that the co-operatives should function in a favourable economic and legal environment.
5. Finally, it should be useful to consider the desirability of establishing in countries where they do not already exist, national- level institutions of co-operatives responsible for assisting in the task of improving the operational efficiency of co-operatives. Such institutions could undertake (i) studies of existing operational methods and procedures at national and/or regional levels in order to evolve improved methods and procedures, (ii) to make available to the co-operatives on short-term basis-four to eight weeks-trained personnel who would study on the spot the operational methods and problems of a co-operative and suggest ways of effective improvements, (iii) to assist the staff of the co-operative in the adoption of recommended practices and producers.

Therefore, co-operative credit structure may be emphasised for agricultural development. Henry Wolf has rightly brought out the role of credit in agricultural development stating without agriculture, co-operation would in India lose its chiefest field of action. And without co-operation agriculture, however well officered, would lose its best instrument to work with.[40]

2.5. Estimation of Agricultural Finance

The credit requirement may connote nothing more than the requirements for credit of borrowers which were met through operations of the credit system and which were reflected in the records of business of cultivators or non-cultivators. The growth of co-operatives in India and Germany took place to meet credit needs of agriculturist. Although credit is highly essential for agricultural transformation, various studies have proved the need for 'bringing the gap between planting and harvest'. But there are regional variations in the demand for credit, because levels of agricultural development, the types of crops grown, stage and adoption of modernisation of agriculture, size of holdings, all these things differ from region to region. The capacity for investment of large farmers is greater, while small holders have lower capacity. The small farmers borrow less due to poverty, subsistence, ignorance and non-viable farming units. In a region where agriculture is more developed, the financial flow remains higher. Besides the need of the credit and its limit are related to the price index of the agricultural commodities in the market. Use of high technology motivates the farmers to borrow high, because of the expected high income from the use of technology. So, credit is the external source of capital for investment necessary for technological transformation. "The farmer, short of capital for his farm decides, whether he could make more money (or derive more satisfaction) by using part or all of his capital in non-farm business ventures. The farmer with surplus capital faces this same question plus the problem of whether the surplus capital will earn more or less in the farm business than in non-farm business ventures. It is assumed that the farm business can be expected to make use of the funds if that alternative is determined to be most profitable."[41] This is because the demand for loans depends upon the profitability of credit use. The necessary and sufficient condition for investment to be financed through credit is, therefore, that the expected rate of profit should be higher than the sum of market rate of interest *(i.e.* direct cost of credit) plus a discount rate to account for uncertain future *(i.e.* indirect cost of credit)[42] The need of credit also depends upon the season of production. Specially during period between June to December the need for credit remains high. With the beginning of harvesting, farmer's demand for credit declines. Farmers need loans for preparation of land, planting and maintenance of crops. Therefore, the supply of credit has to be "need and production potential based instead of asset or security oriented."[43]

The following information gives an idea of growth of the volume of indebtedness since 1875 calculated by various authorities:

Year	Amount of Debt.		Authority
1875	Rs 371 per occupant		Deccan Riots Committee
1880	1 /3 of land holders in debt, another 1/3 in debt with power to redeem		Famine Committee
1895	45 crores		F. Nicholson
1911	300*	"	Edward Maclagan
1924	600	"	M.L. Darling
1930	900	"	Central Banking Enquiry Committee
1935	1200	"	P.J. Thomas

*The estimate relates to Madras only and on the basis of that estimate Sir Edward Maclagan arrived at the figure of ₹ 300 crores for all India.

Source: Agricultural Finance in India (with Special reference to Co-operative Movement), D.K. Rangnekar, Co-operators Book Depot, Bombay, 1952, p. 69.

Besides, the various committees and working groups of Government Agencies and RBI have estimated the credit requirement for our agriculture purposes. The details are given below:

Year	Credit need estimation	Authority
1951-52	₹ 750 Crores	A.I.R.C.S.C.
1961-62	₹ 1034 Crores	A.I.R.D.I.S.
1969	₹ 2000 Crores	A.I.R.C.R.C.
1969	₹ 2500 Crores	Working Group of (N.C.C.)
1970-71	₹ 1623 Crores	N.CA.E.R.
1970-71	₹ 14210 Crores	A.I.R.C.R.C.(RBI)
1976	₹ 9400 Crores	N.C.A.
1978-79.	₹ 3000 Crores	Sub-group on agricultural credit for the group of co-operative for 5th plan.
1985	₹ 16,549 Crores	N.C.A.
1989-90	₹ 14,585 Crores	7th Plan Projection
2000-2001	₹ 1430,767* lakhs	
ST	₹ 10,70,682 lakhs	7th Plan Projection
MT	₹ 2,11,871 lakhs	7th Plan Projection
LT	₹ 1,48,214 lakhs	7th Plan Projection

*Co-operative credit

Source: 1. Rural Banking in India: S.S.M. Desai, p. 39.
2. Kurukshetra — Vol. XXX, No. 2, Oct. 16, 1980, p. 9.

D.K. Desai[44] in his keynote address Illustrated the financial requirement at all India level according to size of holding (see Table 2.8). Both cash and kind expenditure and cash and kind expenditure plus imputed value of family labour are in same ratio to almost all size of farms. The credit requirement to small and marginal farms will rise from 26.26 per cent of total requirement in 1984-85 to 29 per cent in 2000 A.D. So, during this period the rise will be about 3 per cent which the share of medium farm will be at 52.93 per cent of total requirement in 2000 A.D. which was 50.93 per cent in 1984-85. The share of large farms in total requirement will fall from 22,81 per cent in 1984-85 to 19.01 per cent in 2000 A.D. So, major share of credit is harnessed by medium farms size group.

Year		Total	SF and MF	MdF	LF
1984-85					
	C 1	29,464	7,740	15,003	6,722
	C 2	36,011	9,460	18337	8,214
1990					
	C 1	34,156	9,892	17,771	6,493
	C 2	41,747	12,090	21,721	7,936
1995					
	C 1	40,567	11,748	21,107	7,712
	C 2	49,582	14,359	25,798	9,425
2000					
	C 1	49,356	14,293	25,680	9,383
	C 2	60,324	17,470	31,386	11,468

Table No. 2.8: Financial Requirement at All India Level According to Size of Holding

(₹ Crores)

C 1 = Cash and kind expenditure.
C 2 = Cash and kind expenditure plus inputed value of family labour.

> "The reduction of financial requirement of the large group in 1990 compared to 1984-85 is due to the reduction in the proportion of the operated area."

Before World War II rural indebtedness was about ₹ 1800 crores, out of which nearly ₹ 900 crores were required for repaying old debts. During 1951-52 all India average borrowing per household remained between ₹ 160 to ₹ 210 for cultivator households and ₹ 66 for non-cultivator households. Average borrowing per rural household was in the range of ₹ 309 to ₹ 358 for cultivator borrowing and ₹ **171** for non-cultivators borrowings. There was region-wise (or state-wise) variation in the demand for credit because of differences in the stage of agricultural development, types of crops grown, stage of modernisation of agriculture and availability of finance from private and institutional credit etc. 47 per cent of the total borrowing was for consumption purposes, 32 per cent for capital expenditure on farms, and 11 per cent for current cultivation expenditure on farms. During 1961-62, 52 per cent of borrowers were cultivators, and 72 per cent of borrowers belonged to the lowest asset group of ₹ 500 and less, who borrow for meeting family expenditure. Total borrowings declined from 59 per cent of the family expenditure in 1951-52 to 52 per cent in 1961-62 and the quantity of debt rose from ₹ 526 to ₹ 708 in the same period. This was because of the rise in demand for better seeds and manures. Fertilizer Association of India's report of the Fertilizer Committee (1968), estimated credit requirement for fertilizer and pesticides at ₹ 347 crores for 1970-71. The MCA has estimated the credit requirement of the farm sector to be ₹ 16,549 crores by 1985, but the actual credit advanced for the year 1984-85 was 5456 crores which formed 58 per cent of the estimated credit requirement by the NCA. By 1984-85 commercial banks were expected to meet 50 per cent of the total credit requirement.

However, the estimation of credit requirement of rural families presents a difficult problem which may be considered in two stages. First, there is the problem of defining the concept of credit requirement and secondly that of actually estimating the same from the available data. Estimation of credit need is better done by PACS at micro-level, it also facilitates the estimation of credit need at macro-hold contact which the co-operatives have.

2.6. Some Issues of the Present System

Credit to any section of the society or any sector of the economy is a means of development not an end in itself. A provision of agricultural credit to low income people with poor educational background is not generally warranted. But it is generally accepted that, farmers can become a productive unit only when they have been given the money or capital or financial input. Indeed it is an essential part of their farming life. A major task is to discipline credit, and particularly to educate the farmers in farm business with commercial calculations. In underdeveloped countries everybody, every sector needs credit, and the lending agencies may be lacking due to their inability to provide the required credit supply due to the economic backwardness in all respects, yet, credit should be a privilege. C.J. Howse[45], notes, "credit is a privilege, not everyone's right and that privilege must be earned. The greatest need today is for a system that teaches peasant farmers how to develop by using the resources they already have and that gives them confidence in their own ability to affect their status in society." Credit is thus a lubrication to wheels of development, which helps pleasant functioning of the wheels.

But the present system of agricultural finance is somewhat confused and is not a failure in respect. Some problems still unanswered, are also found.

2.6.1. Credit Requirement

Credit requirement plans should be a strategical aspect of a planned economy of a country. A borrower's credit requirements should have to be measured for developmental planning. But it is a common observation that, the required loan amount is always not available to farmers, because a lender concentrates on the economics of the farmer whom he lends while a borrower borrows in the name of business but uses the amount for his family expenses. Generally, a borrower from underdeveloped region or economy thinks his family needs more important than those instead of farm business. This tendency may provide an opportunity to corruption in lending business. And this is what is happening in rural credit operations. Only estimation of credit at macro level (*i.e.* sectoral level) is not enough, but a farmer's requirements either for his family or for his farm business should also be assessed. An even if so estimated, the estimated amount may not reach the target. For example, the

NCA had estimated the credit requirement at ₹ 16549 crores by 1985 at full programme, and at the graduated level it was ₹ 9400 crores. The actual credit advanced for the year 1984-85 was ₹ 5456 crores which formed 58 per cent of the estimated credit requirement by the NCA.[46] Although estimation of credit requirement is a tough task, as it defers according to the farm activity, soil, climate, crop, size of holding and regions, etc. However it should be emphasised taking into its scope the agricultural system.

D.K. Desai has recommended some points in connection with institutional credit requirements for agricultural production at 2000 A.D.:

1. The credit requirements for agriculture should take to account not only credit needs of the agricultural production subsystem but also of the whole agricultural system.
2. It should include credit required for input distribution from factory to farm, considering the wholesale and retail prices.
3. It should include agro-processing industries, and should get some priority.
4. High priority should be given to short-term credits. The present system should be reviewed.

Thus credit system needs to be reviewed, revised and if possible another alternative should be put forth.

2.6.2. *Institutional Chaos*

Multi-agency approach has created a mere chaos in their functioning. Commercial banks have to allot 40 per cent of total credit to priority sector because of the policy of the Central Govt. but they do not consider agriculture as credit-worthy to finance. Branches of commercial banks are operating at a lower business level in rural area. The RRBs are in transit. The share of co-operatives is declining since the entrance of commercial banks. Indeed they are competing with each other. As commercial banks belong to public sector, their employees' efficiency is controversial. They are unable to maintain the golden touch with the local needs and borrowers. Co-operatives are eligible but lack in carrying out bank business. They are only credit disbursing agents. Moreover, credit limit constrains the functioning of local co-operative agencies. The system of bhishis has recently emerged to fulfil the local needs. Their functioning is like a collective/co-operative money lending business, but they charge 5 per cent rate of interest per month. In south-eastern part of Maharashtra and south-northern part of Karnataka almost every village has one or two Bhishi Mandals, Farmer borrow both from commercial banks and co-operative societies too. If necessary they even dare to borrow lavishly from local non-institutional agents. And, therefore, repayment becomes difficult or it has to be adjusted with new borrowings. Thus there is a special institutional need to fulfil the cent-per cent requirements of agricultural finance, like industrial sector which has various institutions for financing industrial purposes.

2.6.3. *Indebtedness*

Though money market is sufficiently extensive non-institutional indebtedness is a major problem in rural area. Only a shift from non-institutional to institutional credit borrowing has occurred during the post-independence period. According to Debt and Investment Survey report, in 1971,42.81 per cent of the rural house-holds reported outstanding loans from both institutional and non-institutional sources. The proportion declined to 19.97 per cent in 1981. Though the essential total number of rural households increased from 77.04 million to 93.62 million between 1971 and 1981, a decline of this order in the proportion of indebted households implies a reduction in the absolute number of indebted households from 32.98 million in 1971 to 18.70 million in 1981 *i.e.* a decline of the order of 43.30 per cent over the decade. If this goes on declining, then what because of lending agencies? Who will borrow from lending agencies? But a few case studies depict the fact that, about 80 to 85 per cent households in agriculturally developed area are indebted during 1984-85.[48] The ratio of indebtedness is illustrated in Table No. 2.9. Govt. is also emphasising the farm credit. But the question is: is indebtedness a good symptom?

Table No. 2.9: Indebtedness in Shirol Tehsil

Agencies	% of Borrowed Amount	% of Borrowers
Money-lenders	6.62	6.68
Traders	0.02	0.23
Relatives and Friends	4.66	9.21
Commercial Banks	33.69	20.27
Co-operatives	55.04	62.90
Others	6.53	6.69
Total	100.00	100.00

2.6.4. Habit of Borrowing

Usually farmers borrow according to their economic status. Sometime, overcreditisation may occur, where repayment becomes very difficult. Undercreditisation may be automatically handled. But the universal truth is that a farmer has to borrow for his economic development. A repayable amount always keeps both lender and borrower very safe, and it should be welcomed. But it is very hard to identify the break-even-point between lender's lendable and borrower's repayable amount. That is why a credit agency should know attitudes of borrowing. Particularly, in an underdeveloped economies such habit or overcreditisation does occur, because the demand for credit is higher than its supply.

2.6.5. Renewal of Debts

When repayment becomes difficult or is not possible, the borrowed loan may be categorised into overdues; disagreeable factor to the lending agencies. Therefore, banking agents force the borrower to repay. Instead of permanent repayment of loans, farmers tend to renew the loans. Renewal of debt may be categorised into two: (a) when a borrower has no capacity to repay due to variety of reasons, he has to adjust the renewal of loans by temporarily borrowing from non-institutional agencies. After applying for the fresh loan. Part or whole of the sanctioned loan would again be used for repaying the non-institutional debt, (b) when repayment of borrowed amount is not possible, a borrower farmer, if banking agent agree, may pay only the interest for the year. Such type of renewals is always practised by many people.

2.6.6 Credit to only Creditworthy Borrowers

Credit is being provided only to the creditworthy borrower farmer. What about non-creditworthy? From whom do they seek the loans? They have to depend on non-institutional agencies, for which they have to suffer humiliation, indulge in sycophancy and, to certain extent exploitation (both psychological and economic). The landless agricultural labours and artisans have no creditworthiness. They should also get some facilities, though not as a right.

2.6.7. Role of Co-operatives

Co-operative is the very hope of rurality's. If it fails, the very hope of ruralites will die. But the major benefit is being harnessed by well-to-do people. It is also observed in a state like Maharashtra that, the movement is spreading in urban than in rural area. Farmers are very much dependent on co-operatives. But co-operatives face the shortages of funds. Apart from this, more often than not, the well off and the vocal, rural section with their clouts of various hues are the major beneficiaries or rural credit facilities offered. This trend has to be reversed. The share of co-operatives is decreasing in the total disbursement of loans. The scheme of adoption of villages by commercial bank, under the 20-point programmes are held responsible for the disappearance of PACS. Borrowers rush towards such commercial banks because of the bonanza of various facilities. Besides the overdues are growing in co-operative rural credit sector. Credit exemption scheme of some states has created policy problems of money market.

Doubtlessly, co-operatives, no doubt have to abide by rural attachment, and have a special hierarchy from top to bottom. It is the only hope of rural development if directed in a more desirable way. It is necessary to trim the staff to make them work-oriented and not mere employment-oriented as they have often become.

It, therefore follows that, the agricultural credit should be safe, cheap and it should educate the farmers in farm business. A credit institution should be structurally sound and should have the ability to generate its own profits, ability to take care of (a) expenses for developing its business, (b) supervision of end-use of credit, (c) training and effective supervision of staff and (d) other incidental liabilities including provisions for bad and doubtful debts. That is why we suggested CVBs at last.

Notes and References

1. Mosher, A.T., Getting Agriculture Moving, Agricultural Development Council (Fedrick A. Praeger Publishers), New York, 1968, p. 161.
2. *Ibid.*, p. 121.
3. Bringer, G.K., Structure of Capital Market in Capital and Credit Needs in Changing Agriculture, (ed.) Baum E.L. Harword G.D. and Heady E.O. The Iowa State University Press, IOWA, USA 1961.
4. Daniel, A.V., *op. cit.*, p. 57-58.
5. Sharma, R.D., Agricultural Finance in India 1980, p. 16, 17.
6. Kahlon, A.S., Modernisation of Punjab Agriculture, Allied Publishers, 1984, p. 18.
7. Mehta, S.C., Agricultural Credit Mobilisation and Allocation, with special reference to District Jhabua (M.P.), Vora Publishers and Distributors, Allahabad, 1987, p. 3.
8. MacClelland, David, The Achievement Motive in Economic Growth, p. 93.
9. Mamoria, C.B. and Saksena, R.D., Co-operation in India, Kitab Mahal, 1983, p. 15.
10. *Ibid.*, p. 15, 16.
11. Mehta, S.C., *op. cit.*, p. 55, 56.
12. Jugale, V.B., Socio-Economic and Technological Impact of Co-operative Credit on Agriculture, Ph.D. Thesis (unpublished), Shivaji University, Kolhapur, 1987.
13. Rana, R.P., Agrarian Revolt in Northern India, during the last 17th and early 18th centuries Indian Economic and Social History Review, Vol. XVIII, Nos. 3 and 4, July. Dec. 1981, p. 287-326.
14. Roy, Choudary, Tapan, Agrarian System of Mughal India, Enquiry, Spring 1965, 97, 99 and Irfan Habib referred by Rana R.P.
15. Singh, Dilbagh, Caste and the Structure, p. 299, 311 referred by Rana R.P.
16. Singh, Dilbagh, *opt. cit.* and Satish Chandra, Some Aspects of Indian Village Society, p. 51, 54 both referred by Rana R.P.

17. Huberman Leo, Man's Worldly Goods, 1936.
18. Deccan Riots Report, p. 49.
19. Report of the Agricultural Finance, Sub-Committee, 1945, RBI, 1965, p. 5.
20. *Ibid.*, p. 5.
21. Report of the Economist, Govt. of Madras, 1946.
22. One bigha = 0.1638404 hectare.
23. Sudi Arzadasht dt. Kati, 10.V.S. 1751/1694 referred in Rana R.P. *opt. cit.*, p. 301.
24. A document granting concessions in revenue rates.
25. Catanack, I.J., Rural Credit in Western India: Rural Credit and Co-op. Movement in Bombay Presidency, 1875-1930, University of California Press, 1970.
26. Memoria, C.B. and Saksena, R.D., *opt. cit.*, p. 123.
27. Petition of the inhabitants of Poona assembled in public meeting held on 7th July, 1901 to Governor, Bombay. I.O.R. Bombay Legislative Proceedings, Vol. 6237, referred by Catanack, I.J., *opt. cit.*, p, 41.
28. Annual Reports of NABARD and the erstwhile ARC and ARDC. Quoted UAE, Vol. 41, No. 4 Oct.-Dec. 1986, p. 565.
29. Raj Krishna, Next Phases of Rural Development, Seminar, 28th August, 1978.
30. Joshi, Shyam, Bank Karje, Dhoranancha Phervichar Avashyak (Marathi), Maharashtra Times daily, 25-2-1987.
31. Shrishrimal, W.C., Co-operative Economy: Problems and Potentialities, The Maharashtra State Co-op. Bank Ltd., Bombay, 1978, p. 19.
32. Nanjundaiya B., EPW, Sept. 26, 1987.
33. *Ibid.*
34. Vaikunth Mehta National Institute of Co-operative Management — Co-operation — An Interdisciplinary Approach: Proceedings of a Seminar, 1969.
35. Saxena, K.K. Evolution of Co-operative Thought, Somaiya Publications Pvt. Ltd., 1974, p. 11.
36. See Issawi Charles, Egypt at Mid-Century, 1954.
37. RBI., Working Group on Multi-agency Approach in Agricultural Finance 1978, p.7
38. Inaugural Address to the Fourth Indian Co-operative Congress, Nov. 29, 1963.

39. Singh, Mohinder, Agricultural Co-operative Credit in Asia, in Agricultural Co-operative Credit in South-East Asia (ed) ICA, p. 10, 11.
40. Naidu, Tirupati V., Farm Credit and Co-operatives in India, Vora & Co. Publishers Pvt. Ltd., 1968, p. 85.
41. Nelson, A.N., Credit as a Tool for Agricultural Producer — N. Cent. Reg. Publ. No. 4 and Great Plains Agricultural Council, Publi. No. 15, 1957, p. 10.
42. Singh, Baldev, Role of Credit in Agricultural Development, A Case Study of a Backward Indian District Surendernagar, Anvesak, Vol. II, No. l, June 1977, p. 16.
43. Desai, D.M. and Desai, D.K., Farm Production Credit in Changing Agriculture, IIM, Ahmedabad, 1971, p. 74.
44. Desai, D.K., Institutional Credit Requirement for Agricultural Production — 2000 A.D. Keynote paper, 48th Annual Conference held at B.H.U., 27-29 Dec. 1988, p. UAE, Vol. 43, No. 3, July-Sept, 1988, p. 341.
45. Howse, C.J., Agricultural Development Without Credit, Agricultural Administration, Vol. I, 1974, p. 259-62.
46. Desai, D.K., Institutional Credit Requirements for Agricultural Production — 2000 A.D., UAE, Vol. 43, No. 3, July-Sept. 1988, p. 351.
47. *Ibid.,* p. 350.
48. Jugale, V.B., *op. cit.*

3

Theories of Agricultural Finance

Efficient use of capital either in Industrial activities or in agricultural activities may be testified by a qualitative change in functioning of the system and quantitative change in the result of functioning. The use of capital is determined by the terms and conditions on which it is obtained. Borrowed capital needs to be efficiently used, which should motivate the borrower to achieve higher yields and save more. A part of the savings is diverted towards working capital or current production needs, while the long-term savings are made available for investments as fixed capital in agriculture. Working capital includes annual financial requirements for production expenses and the net cumulative seasonal financing requirements for the family support. The investment in agriculture later enters into the agriculture, boosting agricultural yield for a long period. The deficiency in working capital due to unavoidable circumstances makes it inevitable to borrow. This borrowing takes place with a great care and cautions. Nicholson observed, "The lesson of universal agrarian history from Rome to Scotland is that an essential of agriculture is credit. Neither the condition of the country nor the nature of the land tenures, nor the position of agriculture affects the one great fact that agriculturists must borrow."[1] Agriculture needs credit because agriculture is an anthropological activity, and it is a big business. And a business needs financing, which should be handled on a profit motive basis. The finances provided for agricultural activities is called as agricultural finance. It relates to both macro- and micro-financing aspects of agricultural segment of the economy. "Macro-finance is concerned primarily with (a) the amount of capital to be allocated to agriculture; the terms and conditions under which it is made available, and the way in which it is used in the aggregate sense of balanced production economic efficiency and the like."[2] Macro-financing also includes, the institutional and non-institutional credit policies, rate of interest, Government's priority to agriculture Central Bank's policy in respect of agricultural finance, urge and need of agricultural development, loaning programmes of the institutions, state's legislations, supervisory agencies like LIC, Central Banks, Government etc. "The micro-financing aspect of agricultural finance pertains to the individual farm, which includes those parts of farm management related to the acquisition, and the use of capital in farm business."[3] This aspect consists of the choice of credit institution, types of loans (short-term, medium-term and long-term), purposes of credit, amount of capital needed and its utilisation, security to be pledged, mode and arrangements of repayment etc.

Farm capital requirements may be provided either by internal sources or external sources. Internal financing is a direct investment through the income stream of individual farm family, and external financing includes credit, where credit is a device for facilitating the temporary transfer of purchasing power from an individual or organisation to another, Credit provides the basis for increased production efficiency through specialisation of function.[4] External financing requires a systematic approach for revitalisation of agriculture. Special policy and priority measures should be adopted for agricultural growth, because it experiences totally different problems compared with other sectors. Agricultural growth[5] (development[6] and progress[7]) has various facets, which can be assessed separately. Our agriculture being backward and individualistic, faces various institutional and lion-institutional problems and is dependent on nature, and is riddled with outmoded technology. All these considerations make it imperative to restructure agricultural credit policy in an innovative spirit. With these objectives in mind, it becomes necessary to examine critically various approaches towards the theory of agricultural finance.

3.1. Risk and Uncertainty Theory of A.F.

The risk and uncertainty concepts in agriculture are subjects internationally discussed by theoretical economists and empirical analyists.[8] The operations of a farm enterprise are not as protected as in the case of commercial and industrial enterprises.

Forecasting in non-agricultural enterprises is practised, but the forecasting of farm income is a difficult task. Agriculture suffers from various risks and uncertainties. For example, (i) the risks, emanating from natural hazards and calamities, such as earthquakes, floods, droughts, famines, hail-storms, tornados, damage of crops due to pests, insects and other diseases, or loss of cattle due to accidents and infectious diseases etc., (ii) the risks of loss of property by fire, thefts and burglary etc., loss due to abrupt and wide fluctuations in prices of farm products, the risk arising out of the death or disability of the farmer.[9]

Credit risk is one of the basic aspects in the economic success or failure of both the lenders and the borrowers, not just an abstract summary of project loan proposal, characterised and invented by theoreticians and/or lending practitioners. It is a factor that is constantly and continuously considered and evaluated in the marketplace. Credit risk is faced both by lenders and borrowers. It is indeed a managerial business of both agencies to tackle according to their own abilities, "Retrospectively, credit risk is measured by actual credit difficulties recorded after the fact delinquencies, foreclosures, losses etc. Prospective credit risk, which looks ahead to the future probability of credit difficulties is often measured by the movements of those loan and borrower characteristics that are known to be related to credit difficulties. Such characteristics as repayments to income ratios, maturities and loan to value ration."[10] Thus implicit risks rendered both by lenders and borrowers of agricultural finance have to be tackled through efficient and skilled managerial administration. Lender has to administer the risk, while borrower has to manipulate the income-loan ratio or asset-loan ratio on a prospective managerial gut. A lender's business is 'selling' credit and loan services in a competitive market and this fact has an important bearing on his loan and service policies. The lending policy depends on the factors like procedures in loan application and disbursement, loan amount, security and valuation, supervision, treatment of customers, repayment of loan and its expectation, loan recovery, risk bearing, and characteristics of loanees and witnesses etc. Farm finance management among farm management techniques has various dimensions which should be dealt with while lending to agriculturists. Moreover, all this has also to work in the framework of policies of Central Bank and the Government. Thus the problem is of balancing risks and benefits, of balancing the cost involved in reducing credit risk against the benefits derived from such a reduction, and of balancing the costs of increasing credit risk against the benefits derived from the increase.[11]

Apart from risks emanating from physical as well as natural factors, borrowers have to face unexpected financial losses arising out of low income and other unforeseen natural occurrences and fluctuations. An increase in farm investment will take place only when the risks and uncertainties in the minds of farmers are removed. The borrowers' risk is greater than that of the lenders' risk. The lender as a seller of credit always tries to keep himself safe in lending practices by way of security, supervision, keeping reserve funds etc. Therefore, the lender is safer than the borrower. Borrowers have to bear natural risks, fluctuations of prices of farm products as well as technical risks. "Three types of changes occur over time in the risk position of the economy and in the location of its peril points. First, there is the variation that takes place within the business cycle. Credit risk varies in response to the cyclical movements of the economy and associated with cyclical changes in production, incomes, and employment. Second, credit risk will vary with long run changes in the degree of economic stability. These might be due to secular shifts in the industrial structure or the occupational make-up of the economy or they might be due to governmental actions, either through the so-called automatic stabilizers or by discretionary economic policy actions. Third, related to both cyclical stability and credit risk, institutional changes take place in the credit markets. The spread of repayment amortisation has been among the more important of these."[12]

Therefore it is essential to increase the risk bearing abilities of both lenders and borrowers. Risk bearing ability means ability to accept unexpected low income and unpredictable losses and expenses and continue in farming. It is made up of mainly of five things; (1) ability to make and save money, (2) stability and reliability of income, (3) ability to borrow in both good and poor times, (4) ability to reduce operating and living expenses in poor periods, (5) own funds — the backbone of risk bearing ability.[13] The fear of debt should have to be removed from the minds of the farmers. Some farmers fear to be in debt. Debt, they feel, is a malignant disease which keeps them always in debt. But now-a-days some farmers bear this risk of borrowing credit for effective yield of agricultural production, Fear of debt has been a factor in management decisions of farmers for a long time. In some cases farmers expressed this fear by a feeling that it was something to be avoided at almost any cost. This view was expressed long ago by Shakespeare in the following words:

Neither a borrower nor a lender be,
For loan oft, loses both itself and friend.[14]

To overcome the fear of being in debt, farm educational programmes should be provided to bring the awareness about usefulness of credit and better credit utilisation.

It is said that borrowing dulls the edge of husbandry. However, credit is an important input for increasing agricultural output. The need of the hour may be to strengthen the risk bearing abilities by the lenders and borrowers. The lenders' risk may be minimised by linking credit with marketing[(x1)], coinciding with time of payment[(x2)], motivate the borrowers to pay the loan by building personal relations.[(x3)], supervision over credit utilisation,[(x4)] meeting market imperfection by keeping reserve funds,[(x5)] involving outsides partner by supplying seeds, fertilizers and implements.[(x6)] (1) Marketing link with credit is only possible when both agencies are fully developed and efficiently managed.

$$LR = f(x1, x2, x3, x4, x5, x6)$$

The market agency should be able to harness the marketable surplus from farmers. A credit agency will be safe if the borrowed money is used for cash crops and cash crops have a market link either to direct market yards or to the processing activities. In some parts of western Maharashtra, where sugarcane is grown in large amount and supplied to the co-operative sugar factories, the credit agencies (particularly co-operative credit) are working in an efficient manner. The co-operative agencies have horizontally and vertically linked with various farm activities in rural areas. Thus if both credit and marketing agencies are viable to tackle respective problems faced by farmers, only the risk bearing capacities of both agencies will be strengthened, and will dare to solve the problems, (2) Time to time borrowing and repayment strengthens the risk bearing ability and goodwill among credit agencies. When borrower purchases the loan, he has to manage it, to increase income levels and income sources. So that repayment becomes easy and safe. Dues always creates obstacles in selling and purchasing of credit. That is why an emphasis should be given to the classification of credit according to period and cause. A coincidence of cause and period will strengthen the risk bearing abilities of both lender and borrowers. However, provision of timely credit supply is essential in agriculture business. It was explained by Cato during the 2nd century B.C. that, if you are late in (agricultural) decisions, then you will probably be late in almost all fronts of economic development. (3) Thirdly, credit agencies can build personal relations with borrowers, which helps to mobilise the small savings and repayment of borrowed loans. The development and growth of urban co-operative credit movement is successful because of its local contacts and local needs. Public sector banks lack in local contacts and local relations. In a country like ours, such relations motivate the farmers psychologically, strengthens the risk and uncertainty bearing abilities of farmer borrowers. (4) Supervision over credit utilisation is a businesslike phenomenon which may be a fulcrum to the credit agency. But morally it may hinder the borrowers and they may not feel free in their productive activities. So, it is a fastidious co-efficient related to credit. However, a skilled banker may use this weapon on an efficient manner, without causing evil or harm to the borrower farmers. (5) Economically, it is worthwhile to strengthen the reserve funds so as to meet the market imperfections. The market imperfections are more active in underdeveloped countries than in developed countries. However, credit supply may create perfection both in resource utilisation *i.e.* production sector and consumption. But there are certain limitations of keeping reserve funds. Indeed it is dependent on the turnover of credit agency. No credit agency will not maintain the reserve fund fully at its initial stages. It is slowly growing. (6) Lastly, credit agencies have to keep relations with the outside partners like, seeds, fertilizers, implements and other input supplying agencies, as, such inputs help to produce more, through which a surety of repayment will be created.

Such integration of factors strengthens the risk bearing abilities of lending agencies. And these are possibly managed by a credit agency without harming the borrower. Thus organised sector has to build the relations like that of non-institutional instruments of credit supply. But Government policies should come to rescue, emphasising the increased risk bearing capacities of lending agencies. Nationalisation of 20 commercial bank is a step in this way. Still, there is need to strengthen the risk bearing abilities of lending agencies through appropriate Government policies.

A borrower always goes on borrowing if there is facility available to borrow, without caring about repayment capacity if he is in needy situations. Particularly, a borrower of underdeveloped countries has to fulfil a variety of needs both from households and farm sectors. Although a borrower will have to borrow according to his borrowing capacity, a borrower of an underdeveloped country like ours has leased or no creditworthiness for borrowings, even developed. So, credit is a must to develop both farmers and farm activities. Though a borrower goes on borrowing loans, because of the facility, they have to prepare or arrange to repay the same. Sometime a borrower has to bear risks in credit business. In India, where agriculture is still dependent on nature, the risk and uncertainty bearing capacities of credit borrowings lack among farmers. However, borrower's risk bearing ability may be strengthened by:

1. Taking up less risky or more stable farm enterprises:
2. Diversification of production;
3. Flexible production programmes and processes;
4. Better plant protection and other farm practices which would reduce losses and increase returns;
5. Crop insurance and other insurances;
6. Forward contracts for product sales and input purchases;
7. Building up personal credit through fair dealings; and
8. Practising savings and reduction of expenses and building up of equity.[15]

In a scanty rainfall area, crop expectation may be increased by proper land tilling, scientific preparation of land for cultivation, choice of crops, crop combination, timely sowing and eradication of weeds properly. Along with this, basically, to strengthen the risk, borrower have to use HVVP seeds, bio-chemicals and mechanical technologies, irrigation, and managerial skill of farm activities etc. All these factors strengthen the risk bearing abilities of borrowers, So, what is necessary is proper farm management skills which should be developed among the farmers themselves. Therefore, a borrower's risk is dependent on quality of soil(qs), choice of crop (cc), crop protection (cp), use of bio-chemical and mechanical technology (bmt), irrigation (i), marketing (m), family needs(fn), availability of input services (is), family background (fb), and capital oriented or labour oriented investments (cli) etc. Concurrent variable capital investment, which is generally less may have least risk than fixed capital investment.

$$Br = f(qs, cc, cp, bmt, i, m, fn, is, fb, cli)$$

A mere farmer can learn traditional farm practices by deserving others or following his ancestral skills etc. in connection with variable investments, while a fixed capital investment requires to prepare its economics of borrowing and its use for productive purposes. They all are dependent on the rate of returns of investment, which can be computed as follows:

$$Rr = Pp\ (Yi - Yo)/C.$$

Where,

Rr = rate of return of one rupee invested on any concurrent or fixed investment items.

Pp = Price of product.

Yo = Yield of crop without using any concurrent or fixed capital investment.

Yi = Yield of crops obtained by using the concurrent (variable) or fixed capital investments in farm activity.

C = Cost of investment

This probable rate of interest is employed by Cone (1975), which has been used as the profitability criterion because it is easier to compute. Using this criterion Singh and Nautiyal[16] have measured the rate of returns of fertilizer investment in Uttar Pradesh. However, when and how much to borrow depends upon financial stress, assets owned, the reason for which the borrowed amount is being used etc. The financial stress may be calculated as debt to asset ratio. The indicators of financial stress are as under:[17]

1. *The times interest earned ratio:* This is calculated by dividing earnings before interest and taxes by total interest payment.
2. *Financial leverage index:* This is calculated by subtracting farm business expenses less interest payments from net sales by farm business.
3. *Debt burden ratio:* This is calculated by dividing net cash farm income (cash farm business income minus cash farm business expenses) by total farm debt.

A commonly used measure to solvency, the debt-to-asset ratio, reflects the riskiness of farmer's capital structure in terms of the relationship between the capital supplied by farm lenders(debt) and the capital supplied by farmer (equity).[18] The higher the value of the ratio, the greater the degree of financial risk because lenders must be satisfied before equity owners in the event of bankruptcy.

Peter J. Berry and Liden J. Robinson[19] have categorised the risks into two, *viz.*

(a) Business risks,
(b) Financial risks.

Business risk arises from the variability of returns to the investor's risky assets. It is dependent on the financial structure of the invested portfolio. Financial risk arises from the composition and terms of the financial claims on the assets. Any fixed obligation financing as in borrowing and leasing, is considered a form of financial leveraging; it adds to the investor's financial risk. Together, business and financial risks combine to determine total risk. The financial leverage index may be calculated by dividing the return on equity from income by the return on assets from income. If the value of the financial leverage index is greater than one, farmer's earnings per rupee of owned equity capital must necessarily be greater than the earning per rupee on both equity and debt capital. That would suggest that farmers are employing debt capital beneficially (*i.e.*, it represents a net benefit rather than a net cost to them.)

Thus the farm level risk management can be categorised into four types: (a) farm wise (b) crop wise, (c) holding wise (d) natural calamity wise, which differ according to the irrigated, non-irrigated, small and large farm size and food or cash crops etc.

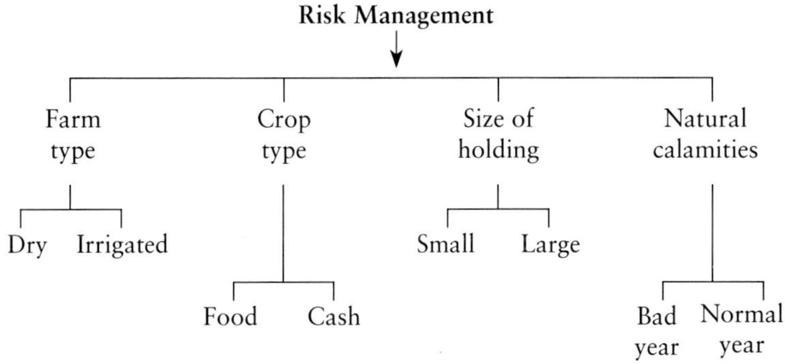

Chart No. 3.1: Risk Management

It is more individualistic than collective or regional. Therefore, it is essential to increase the micro level risk bearing abilities of borrowers, as agriculture is full of individual risks and uncertainties, which have to be systematically minimised, for which, farmers have to acquire entrepreneurial skills in an effective manner. The farmers have to borrow only to the extent of the repayment ease and convenience though risk management by borrowers is a tough task, in comparison with lender's risk but essential to manage. This is better explained by A.G. Nelson in a nice manner indicating red and green lights of agricultural finance. "One would be foolish to load a truck to the point, where an axle would break, if a wheel hit a chuckhole in the road, A farm family would be equally unwise to take on a credit load to the point where they would go 'broke' if adversely hit. Just as some highways have more holes than others, some areas and types of farming involve greater hazards and risks than others. Farmers in high risk areas or with high risk enterprises should take on a lighter debt load in relation to their equity than those in stable areas, or in type of farming where fluctuations in income are relatively small."[20]

3.2. Demand and Supply Theory of Agricultural Finance

Our agriculture has been backward for various reasons. As a result, credit needs are either neglected or remain very small, in comparison with the credit needs of other sectors. Farmer's credit need depends on, (i) his size of operating unit, (ii) his efficiency and farm's productivity, (iii) his control over production and price, (iv) his economic conditions and knowledge of modern technology and (v) need for long-term investment in agriculture etc. Unfortunately, since the operating units in India are small, productivity is low and fluctuations in farmer's control over production and product prices are hedged by various factors. The farmers are poor and ignorant and, therefore, show no interest in long term investments in their agricultural activities.[21] Besides, the great feelings are that, a person who cannot do anything or fails to do any productive work in other sectors, can be absorbed in this core sector; and an illiterate and ignorant person is eligible only to practise agriculture. This is not true today. Moreover, our agriculture undertakes both subsistence and commercial activities. So, the farmers dare to invest in agriculture for long run practices, but they lack in the availability of internal and external funds. However, after independence, various kinds of policy are being introduced to solve the financial constraints meant for agriculture, and the agriculturist dares to invest in it today.

A demand for agricultural finance is dependent on socio-economic and technological background of the farmer's family, and the need is a desire of self-development among farmers. Demand for credit taken for production purposes has no effective burden on agriculturists, because credit improves the production conditions. Production credit is required for concurrent investment in agriculture, for current production, for marketing and other liquid requirements as well as for formation of small assets. The economic gains from production credits are higher and may be acquired in short run. But it may be short-term credit or medium-term credit or long-term credit, which directly and indirectly helps to increase the agricultural production.

Generally, crop loan, which is called as short-term credit is called as production credit. It may comprise concurrent expenses like fertilizers, seeds, labour charges, irrigation charges, light bills etc. Investment purpose comprises, the credit demand for medium and long-term credit investments in agricultural business. Such investment yield (returns) is cumulative in character, because of their durability. And such type of investments differs according to the size of holding. A large farmer can have bigger durables, while a small farmer will hold small quantity of minor implements and assets. Permanent land development or land improvement activities may be categorised as investment in agriculture. For example land levelling, terracing, bindings etc. Consumption credit is essential for effective maintenance of the family as a productive agent in the cultivation and harvesting of crops etc.[22] Consumption purposes like food, cloth, medicine, education, are in a sense, a kind of infrastructure for supporting agricultural activities.

The demand for agricultural credit varies by farm, by region and over time. So, supply according to demand is difficult to predict. Individual demand has been better identified by non-institutional agencies since a few decades. Through an individual contacts, with local environment and individual needs, a lender can get better market to his lending business and he can understand the need by mixing and mingling with local public. There is a variation in the demand for credit according to the season, as there is no future or perspective farming plans due to variety of reasons. They could not prepare a demand schedule, because "demand for credit is determined by liquidity of crop pattern and cropping intensities, size of family — and farm labour, cost of credit and mode of transactions, degree of risk and uncertainties involved in production, marketing inclusive of inventory control and managerial skills. The entire gamut of factors of demand should ultimately depend upon managerial skills, ability and propensities towards risks in agriculture/"[3] Generally demand for credit depends upon main factors like cost of credit, marginal efficiency of credit, repaying capacities, farm production predictability etc.

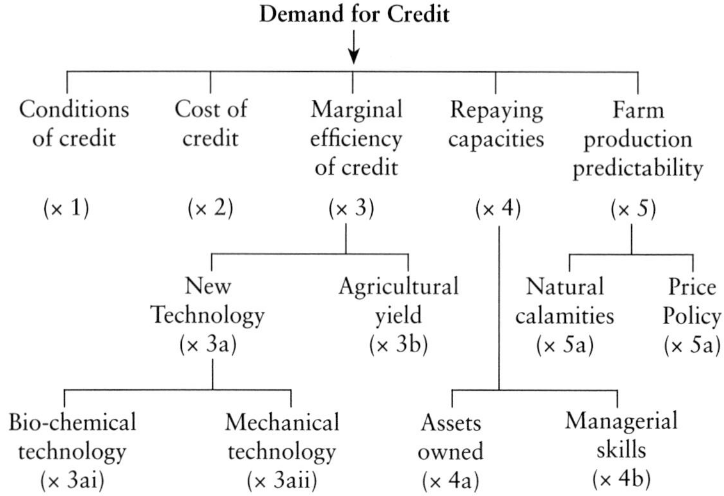

Chart No. 3.2: Demand for Credit

If conditions of credits are easy and the rate of interest is low, the demand for credit will be high. Institutional credit agencies charge low rate of interest but the conditions of the fulfilment documents is difficult to the borrowers. While the non-institutional credit agencies have no conditions of credit, they charge higher rate of interest. Therefore, farmers have to decide according to what is feasible for them. A golden mean between these two, should have to be endorsed, so as to make both ends meet. A credit agency has to be characterised with these two conditions. Marginal efficiency of credit depends on production of new technology and the yield that can be obtained by the adoption of new technology. Marginal efficiency of credit means the marginal efficiency of capital invested with the intension that a rupee invested in a productive activity should gain more. MEC may be defined as, "the productivity of capital or to be more accurate, it may be defined as the highest rate of return over cost accruing from an additional unit of a capital asset" Introduction of new technology will raise marginal efficiency of credit. And the new technology is dependent on the advancement of science, technologies, patentship, competition etc. Technology in agricultural sector may be categorised into two (a) bio-chemical technology which includes the farm items like seeds, fertilizers, pesticides, herbicides, irrigation etc.,

(b) mechanical technology, which includes all implements made by metal, wood, plastic and fibre etc. If a new technology increases the marginal efficiency of credit, the repaying capacity of the borrower farmer will increase. Similarly, if the repaying capacity is high the demand for credit would be high. Repaying capacity depends on the owned assets and managerial skills of the farmer. On the other hand, when farm production is predicted high the credit demand will also be high. And the farm production or yield depends on natural calamities and market structure and policy for agricultural products.

Dc = f (X1, X2, X3, X3a, X3b, X4S X4a, X4b, X5, X5a, X5b)

Using the mathematical explanation, demand for credit is the function of various determinants. The determinant X1 and X2 are guided by Government policy measures. Therefore, these two (X1, X2) factors have only a partial influence. The influence of X3a and X3b is again left to scientists and technologists and the extent of new technology to farmers. When an agriculturist adopts a new technology he will get higher production. Only factors like X5a, X5b are beyond guts and play a vital role in farm business. Specially these conditions should carefully be investigated in the context of a country like ours, so as to strengthen the agricultural credit business.

The supply of credit in varying proportions in respect of various agencies remained the same for a relatively long time. Only the rate of institutional lending agencies has changed, while non-institutional lenders remained at a significant level. Even today money-lenders play a vital role in rural financing. Supply of credit flows from savings and Government grants. In a country like ours, the rate of saving is low in comparison with developed countries. There are various obstacles in raising the saving rate. A part of short-term savings is diverted towards current needs for production and working capital, while long term savings are made available for investment as fixed capital. Thus supply of credit is the function of savings and Government grants.

Sc = f (S, G)

Farmers need to borrow money for their farm activities or allied purposes in order to increase their level of incomes. The lender 1% primarily interested in the security tor his lending or its safe return for which a suitable price is charged by way of interest. The lender always protects his lending responsibility through a pledge of assets, Now-a-days lenders supply variety of loans for short, medium and long period, *e.g.* settlement and development loans, production equipment loans, market loans, secured loans, unsecured loans, cash loans, kind loans etc. Institutional credit mainly depends on either assets or security owned by borrowers or liquidity assets (which can be pledged) with them. All activities of institutional finance are controlled by Government policies while the non-institutional credit is need based. However, such lending is profit oriented. The written documents and certificates are not essential to non-institutional lending procedures. Farmers sometime feel better to borrow from them because non-institutional credit is easy to get, though they charge higher rate of interest. Lending by institutions is governed by rules and procedures which are often found inflexible. Limited liability in the co-operatives and extreme caution and complicated procedures in Government and responsibilities of financial institutions for their depositors have made the supply of credit asset oriented or liquidity based and not need based. Consequently, the supply of credit by institutions is very much limited and the individual money-lenders dominate.[24] Prof. Raj Krishna in his speech on, "Next Phase of Rural Development" (28th August 1978) mentioned that, the paperwork, the travel, the lobbying and the bribing required for getting loans is excessive and often raises the effective cost of institutional credit above the money-lender's interest rates.[25] Recently, a few researches are going to concentrate on this aspect of credit.

Thus supply of agricultural credit is mainly dependent upon the level of savings and capital formation (S1), degree of risk and uncertainties in lending (S2), prospects of financial institutions (S3), and the alternative opportunity for investment (S4). The dominant factor among these determinants is the level of savings, along which other determinants may function.

$$Sc = f(S1, S2, S3, S4)$$

Saving rates are determined on the level of income, propensity to consume and rate of interest on deposits. Higher the income and lower the propensity to consume may result into saving and higher rate of interest on deposits, motivate the saver to save more. Savings always motivate to invest in a higher income earning activities. Once rise in income starts, the forthcoming effects will again cumulate and contribute to the original income. This is how an economy expands with a positive increase in income, savings, investment, capital formation, production, employment etc. Capital formation depends on the level of industrialisation, development of science and technology, and the demand for the manufacturing or industrial commodities. The very process of development activity creates all favourable things for future, but proper strategical plans are desirable to direct development on a proper line. The risk bearing abilities of both lenders and borrowers affect the supply function of credit. One who (lender) bears the risk and uncertainties, can supply funds on a greater scale.

Thus it is always desired to have a balance between demand for and supply of credit for agricultural purposes. Supply of credit should get adjusted with demand for credit instead of target oriented approaches. What is required for a sound agricultural credit system, is the need of stable agricultural credit. Today Government and banking policies are unable to supply credit to the extent of needs of the farmers. Meanwhile, with an effective use of credit, the wealth (asset) of farmers may increase, which might affect their borrowings from banks and institutions. Instead of borrowings they may begin to deposit in banks. In such a situation, there will be no demand agricultural credit. This may create a situation of excess supply of savings without corresponding demand. Therefore demand for and supply of credit requires to be property balanced. Credit should be cheap, but above all safe. State should ensure that agricultural credit is fully institutionalised. As Nicholson observed, "Credit is a weapon that may destroy the unskillful wielder, it is helpful or destructive according as it is used or abused."[26]

3.3. Business *Vs.* Social and Moral Theory of Agricultural Finance

Institutional credit system mainly focuses on the business aspect rather than social and moral aspects of agricultural finance. Profit and loss accounts are kept where business aspect is practised social and moral aspects are disregarded whereas business aspect predominates. But consideration of these social and moral aspects allows a money-lender to remain in business for a long time. It is exactly these factors because of which money-lenders dominate in rural credit even today. Now-a-days the institutional credit agencies give precedence to social aspect for their growth. However, the social and moral aspects of any credit institution differ according to their bureaucratic attitude, interest and efficiency in business. Unfortunately, now-a-days this spirit is absent in majority of businessmen and professionals.

After-all agricultural finance is a business to be practised for the welfare of society. When the business aspect predominates moral responsibility of both creditors and debtors is disregarded. For example, when a money-lender charges a higher rate of interest than the prevailing reasonable rate, then it is obvious that the morality of a money-lender is doubtful. On such occasions farmers can neglect such debt if another source is available, otherwise they can revolt against this attitude of money-lenders. Farmer's revolt against moneylenders in Bombay State during May 1875 at Supa was of this kind. Therefore, the business aspect should not be overemphasised and should be kept within reasonable limits. When business aspect becomes aggressive, the moral and social aspects must be protected by enactment of laws. Particularly so, if the Govt. really believes in the concept of welfare states.

The parameters being used in judging the performance of public sector banks are: (a) growth of deposits, (b) management credit, (c) social banking, (d) compliance with reserve requirements, (e) housekeeping, (f) customer service, and (g) profitability. The parameter like social banking and customer service are emphasised only because of social and moral responsibility of banking business. Bank agency must not forget both depositors and borrowers on whom the bank's business edifice is erected. And because of this that a bank/or manager has to visit potential borrowers through when bank may grow and it is social commitment of all bank employees, indeed to be particular in combining the three aspects of bank administration *i.e.* business and social commitment and moral responsibilities. Because of the combination of these three aspects, the Urban Co-operative Banks and Urban Credit Societies have become very popular. H.P. Prakash Rao[27] has performed an analysis of the profit making and loss incurring branches in relation with various parameters (See Table 3.1).

Parameters	Profit Branches	Loss Branches
1. Avg deposit per branch	42.18	38.01
2. Avg advance per branch	34.65	21.22
3. Avg business per branch (1 + 2)	76.83	59.23
4. Avg staff per branch	6	7
5. Avg business per employee	12.05	8.53
6. Share in total deposits (%)		
(a) Current deposits	3.6	2.0
(b) Savings bank deposits	32.3	29.2
(c) Term deposits	64.1	68.8
7. Share into total advances		
(a) Priority sectors	81.3	79.3
(b) Non-priority sectors	18.7	20.1
8. Income	12.4	11.0
(a) Avg rate of interest earned on advances (%)		
(b) Avg other income of the branch	0.28	0.17
9. Expenditure	7.4	8.4
(a) Avg interest rate on deposits		
(b) Avg salary per employee	0.26	0.27
(c) Salary as % of the avg business	2.1	3.1
(d) Avg other expenditure of a branch	0.36	0.39
10. Avg Profit/loss	1.28	0.59

Table No. 3.1: Performance of Profit-making and Loss-incurring Branches (for the ref. year 1986)

(₹ in lakhs)

He has also identified the special features of loss incurring rural branches which are: (i) those branches operate at a lower business level compared to profit making branches. In other words for the available staff, the branches operate on a lower volume of business, (ii) the income earned from non-fund based business is low as compared to profit branches, (iii) the average rate of interest earned by these branches is low as compared to profit making branches. This may probably be due to blocking of mere loan in non-performing assets, (iv) 'salary' as percentage of average business is comparatively high in the case of loss branches. Moreover, other than business parameters, as mentioned earlier *i.e.* social and moral, if emphasised, the business parameters automatically grows with local relations. Of course bank will not oblige to anyone but *to* develop the business is social commitment and moral responsibility. H.P. Prakash Rao[28] has also mentioned the breakeven business levels at different staff strengths. In table 3.2, he assumed that the branch would be getting the central office interest at the rate of about 3 per cent of its business. Spread is defined as, percentage return on working funds minus percentage interest cost on working funds. And banks profitability can be measured as,

$$\text{Profitability} = \text{Spread}\left(\frac{\text{Operating expenses}}{\text{Average working funds}}\right) \times 100^{29}$$

Staff Strength	4 (1+2 + 1)	5 (1+3 + 1)	6 (1+4 + 1)	7 (2 + 4 + 1)	8 (2 + 5 + 1)
Staff cost	1.05	1.30	1.55	1.90	2.15
Other operating costs	0.30	035	0.40	0.45	0.50
Total operating cost	1.35	1.65	1.95	235	2.65
Less: Other income	0.10	0.15	0.20	0.25	030
Spread	1.15	1.50	1.75	2.10	235
Breakeven level of average business (Avg deposits + Avg advances	38.50	50.00	58.50	70.00	78.50

Table No. 3.2: Breakeven Business Levels at Different Staff Strength

(₹ in lakhs)

and an efficiency rating or ratio may be obtained by:

$$\text{Efficiency Rating or Ratio} = \frac{\text{Profitability}}{\text{Spread}} \times 100^{30}$$

To understand the above formulae it would be useful to define some concepts, which are explained by Parulekar and Ullal[31] They are:

1. Average working fund is equal to the average deposits plus. average borrowing from central office or other banks.

2. $$\text{Cost of Avg. working funds} = \frac{\text{Interest on deposits + interest on borrowings}}{\text{Average working funds}}$$

3. $$\text{Return on Avg. working funds} = \frac{\text{Interest earned on advances + Interest earned on funds lent to central office/Head Office + income from commission exchange and other receipts.}}{\text{Average working funds}} \times 100.$$

After maintaining a minimum business profit, a bank agency must treat agriculture sector as profit earning sector, and automatically both may develop simultaneously. Staff should have to be motivated through proper training or through incentives if possible, for integrating the three major aspects of agricultural finance. Such integration is essential to agriculture, because agriculturists are backward, illiterate, ignorant and traditional. If they are motivated properly, with mobilising their savings as honey-bees collect honey from flowers, and issuing liberal, safe and low cost credit to them, success of bank business can be maintained. That is why agricultural finance in India should have special characteristics and features. Profits may be kept minimum as shown in Table 3.1. And if profits are higher, they may be transferred to loss incurring branches or other bank agencies. Thus, only business motive will not or must not be the end of agricultural finance.

Agricultural finance, devoid of the moral and social aspects, will not be socially acceptable. Farmers must be supplied credit in times of need. Similarly the farmers must arrange for repayment of the loans when conditions improve. For this socially balanced management of agricultural credit, both suppliers and borrowers of credit must behave with social and moral awareness. They should develop a sense of belongingness to the entire system. When this happens, the need for rules, regulations and laws for the practice of agricultural finance will be minimised. In Western countries, balance between economic efficiency and social/ moral restraints has evolved gradually. We should adopt their methods. In a country like India, the integration of these three aspects is essential; because our agricultural financing system is beset with various obstacles. Agricultural finance is in certain areas excessive and some other areas severely inadequate. Only issuing the credit to needy farmers may not serve the purpose. Target oriented attitude of our planners has lost sight of the very purpose of agricultural credit. Unfortunately, even in the co-operative units, where the sense of belongingness to the co-operative society is principally accepted, the percentage and number of defaulters is ever increasing. In many other credit agencies, the business aspect is inefficient and, in many cases, the social aspect is misunderstood according to the interests of the credit agencies. This is observed in co-operative credit, in a more palpable manner. The controversy regarding the business *Vs.* moral aspects of co-operation has mainly centred round the primary agricultural credit societies.[32] V. Timpati Naidu has commented that, "Co-operative is an association of persons and an undertaking. But in India there is a tendency to harp on the social and moral virtues of co-operation to the exclusion of its business efficiency. The social aspect of co-operation is misunderstood and the business aspect is less appreciated if not thoroughly neglected."[33] Commercial banks did not cultivate these attitudes initially. With a small unit it is possible to protect moral/social aspects. It is also essential to keep in view the growth of business aspect. Business efficiency is the core consideration of any credit agency, while in non-credit institutions all aspects are more or less equally important. Their credit business is practised in accordance with need and this exactly is the reason why non-institutional credit agencies continue to dominate even now.

Social and moral aspects mainly comprise: (i) non-profit operation of a firm or agency, (ii) self-help, (iii) brotherhood, (iv) mutual help in any activity, (v) welfare of majority of the people. And the business aspects include: (i) departure from unlimited liability pattern to limited liability pattern with a paid manager, (ii) multi-purpose activities for viability of the institutions, (iii) Government help, (iv) unionisation and vertical integration of agricultural finance institutions etc.

In conclusion we may say that every credit agency must first adhere to efficiency needed by economic considerations and then turn to moral and social aspects of agricultural finance.

Small size credit agencies may find it easier to consider both aspects. Indian banking provides a unique example of blending harmoniously commercial banking with social banking. Especially during the post nationalisation period the conversion of elitist bank into mass banking has balanced the historical distortion. The expansion of branches in rural area, extension of credit at concessional rates of interest, emphasis on weaker sections and coverage of large number of small borrowers is made possible since nationalisation, as a social responsibility. Before that a concept of social control was introduced. Banks today are actively engaged in anti-poverty programme so as to-do-away with the social and economic evils of the country. More emphasis has been put on the prioritisation of credit through proper and objective induced monetary policy of RBI.

3.4. Cost Theory of Agricultural Finance

Cost of agricultural finance include not only rate of interest but other expenses which the farmers have to undertake to obtain credit. These include fees paid for obtaining a copy of land ownership record, travel towards banking units, refreshment during the visits to banks, waste of his labour hours while visiting credit units, expenses on photographs and other charges, etc. These are main items of expenses, involved in a farmer's getting credit. Such type of expenses does not end with the receipt of finance, but continue up to the final repayment of loan instalment. The items like rate of interest, storage charges, costs involved in uncertainty, marketing costs and period of waiting for marketing the agricultural goods after the agricultural harvesting etc. are the costs incurred after receiving the loan amount. Thus costs of agriculture may be classified into two: (1) The costs incurred by a farmer before he receives the loan amount, (2) The direct or indirect costs which a farmer has to bear after receiving the credit. This type of cost is very difficult to measure. But farmers have to incur such expenses. At every stage, farmers have to try, to minimise these costs. This depends upon the skill and tactics of the farmer. Besides all these, a farmer has to confront the uncertain process of agricultural production which makes agriculture a tough task to measure.

In developing countries like India, where both agriculture and agriculturist are backward, mutually causative, the cost of agricultural finances is high in comparison with the marginal returns. Moreover, the macro agricultural policies, agricultural banks and other agencies, lack effective credit planning strategies for timely supply of agricultural finance. Both micro and macro factors influence the increase in the cost of agricultural finance.

Before the acquisition of loan, a farmer has to prepare documents for the purpose of acquiring credit. His application for loan must enclose: (a) a copy of land ownership from land record office as security, which also specifies the crop cultivated for a year; (b) a certificate from sugar factory (for sugarcane crop loan) indicating last year's quantity of supply of sugarcane to the factory, and per hectare average yield in tonnes, (c) no dues certificate from Primary Agricultural Co-operative Society, if a farmer wishes to purchase loan from commercial banks, (d) a copy/copies of recent photographs for agricultural finance from institution like State Bank of Indian-Agricultural Development Scheme of credit to agriculture etc. Farmers have to pay fees for these enclosures. Other expenses include travelling, waste of labour hours, stamp duties etc. Commercial banks are mainly established in cities or towns, so farmers have to travel to the nearest bank office. On an average, a farmer has to make three to four visits to get his loan amount. During these visits he has to spend some labour hours, which otherwise he could use on his farm. After an application for loan, nearly 15 to 30 days are required to receive the amount. In certain credit plans this period is reduced to 5 to 8 days. Thus, it depends upon the type of bank agency and the type of credit. The Land Development Bank in Maharashtra requires 73 days to disburse the subsequent loan instalments to the borrowers because of its 16 stages of credit sanctioning process.[34] Other co-operative credit too, requires more than 3 months to be finally disbursed after receiving the application. In comparison with all credit agencies, the farmers prefer to borrow credit from money-lenders or traders or relatives and friends, despite a high rate of interest.

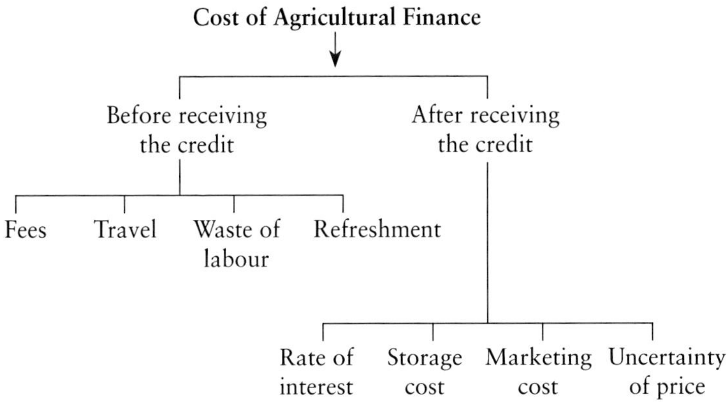

Chart No. 3.3: Cost of Agricultural Finance

Now-a-days the commercial banks have adopted quicker methods/processes of credit disbursement. Naturally the percentage of credit disbursement by commercial banks is more than the co-operatives.[35] All such processes increase the total cost of agricultural finance for the farmers. Such formalities of an unjustified nature create an unfavourable attitude in the minds of farmers towards credit agencies. The following chart will illustrate average cost of agricultural finance before a farmer get the commercial bank's loan amount.

		₹
(i)	Fees of acquiring a copy from land records of ownership	10.00
(ii)	No dues certificate	
(iii)	Travelling (3 times)	20.00
(iv)	Application and revenue stamp or stamp duties	10.00
(v)	Copy of photographs	15.00
(vi)	Cost of labour hours (3 days)	60.00
(vii)	Others	20.00
		Total: 135.00

Certain credit schemes *e.g.* crop loan is dependent on actual plantation of the crop. After planting a particular crop *(e.g.* sugarcane-grapes, betel leaf and the like) a farmer can apply for loan. In such situation, farmers have to borrow local loans for plantation of crops. Apart from this, a farmer has to sign or fulfil various types of forms. Though these may be justified on security and safety grounds, all the complications involved compel the farmers to resort to non-institutional credit agencies.

After the receipt of loan, the first cost that a farmer has to bear is the rate of interest. Then he has to pass through the tensions of uncertainties of nature before he gets the agricultural production. (Here the cost of cultivation is not taken into consideration.) After getting a certain quantity of agricultural production, he has to store and wait for better prices. Here too a farmer has to bear the risk of storage either in his house or else, where he has to face the menace of rats and other rodents as well as grain diseases etc. Alternatively, he has to keep his produce in trader's go down for which he has to pay the go down rents. Finally, he has to face marketing vicissitudes and complexities. Such costs are difficult to measure. Ultimately in certain situations, farmers do not get sufficient return to repay the loan.

In all these activities what is required is better management of both borrowing and repayment of credit for which a farmer has to adjust costs and returns from agriculture in an efficient manner. This is an important aspect of credit among various input management, because the determination of the desirability or practical possibility of changing farm organisation with the help of credit brings desirable change in agriculture. The techniques of marginal analysis can be adopted to determine the optimum combination of various factors or inputs of production.[36] It may be seen that the marginal analysis will compare the costs and returns of a farm enterprise under a scheme of applying successive doses of variable factors keeping other factors constant or fixed. Marginal productivity of credit is higher than any other input in agriculture, because through credit a farmer uses other important inputs for his agriculture.

First, it is essential for the farmer to select the best financing agency. He has to select an agency which minimises his costs and tensions of borrowing. In most cases if a farmer is desirous of borrowing from any other agency, he must follow the method of logical reasoning as to which of the conceivable alternatives will give the best results in their mutual interest. Here, it is assumed that the methods and procedures of credit agencies (institutional and non-institutional) are known to the farmers.

L.J. Norton[37] has evolved certain rules for wiser .use of agricultural credit. They are:

(i) Borrow only in connection with a business which is understood.

(ii) Keep debt at lowest point that permits the business to be large enough to be efficient.

(iii) Study the price level and govern commitments by likely trends in prices during the life of the loan.

(iv) Confine the use of credit to income producing purposes only.

(v) Have a definite programme of repayment.

(vi) Keep debts from getting too high for capital.

(vii) Keep debts from getting too high for income.

(viii) Select a credit agency which will commit in writing to go along when incomes are low.

(ix) Be business-like with a financing agency.

(x) Have an adequate amount of insurance.

However, the use of credit is influenced by factors which are internal and external to the farmers. When the use of capital is restricted by the internal factors it is called internal capital rationing and when restricted by the external factors it is called external capital rationing.[38] The internal capital rationing factors are both socio-psychological and economic in their nature and these factors may be classified into two classes *viz.*: (a) aversion to change,(b) propensity to change.[39]

Both lenders and borrowers try to maximise the yield. Moreover, both try to manage the credit very efficiently. Lending is based on prices at which the loan is deemed, and the cost is also considered with prices. The lender is interested in the items mentioned in *'A'* group and a borrower is always interested in the items mentioned in group *'B'* below:[40]

Group (A)	*Group (B)*
The lender is interested in-	The borrower is interested in-
(a) Making loans which can be collected.	(a) Getting the credit which he can use to advantage or to meet an emergency.

(b) Getting a favourable rate of return on his loan.	(b) Getting credit at reasonable cost.
(c) Obtaining the proper degree of liquidity to fit his own liabilities, if a short-term lender.	(c) Endangering his own assets as little as possible.
(d) Making an adequate volume of loans to keep his funds invested.	(d) Having a favourable repayment principle.
(e) Keeping his costs to a minimum consistent with safety.	(e) Getting credit with a minimum of trouble and "red tape".

If all these tactics are followed in lending and borrowing, the cost will be minimised. Both lenders and borrowers will benefit. A good management must also adhere to the mathematics of borrowing money *i.e.*:

$$I = \frac{PRT}{100}$$

Where,

I = Interest
P = Principle
R = Rate of per cent
T = Time

The formula[41] fitted above may have various possibilities arising out of expected rise in prices, rate of harvest, cost of credit, cost of storage, cost of marketing over a period of time. Generally, a farmer manages such co-relates, and calculates profitability. He always tries to keep cost low and earn profits. If cost overcomes the earnings it shows poor management and if yield overcomes total cost incurred, it shows good management.

Thus, it is clear from the discussion that the cost of credit is a barometer around which various factors revolve. The analysis of cost of credit and returns statements of the borrower provide the answer to the question of estimating his ability to repay the loan. It is also essential to compute the lenders cost of transactions and cost of lending which should be taken into consideration because of the higher cost (direct & indirect) incurred by commercial banks located in rural areas. The R.B.I. particularly, are being managed in rural area are facing this problem. And therefore, they are in doldrum, of course the study of RRBs should have to he specially overviewed. But now the question is that, in spite of the efforts towards large scale vital monetisation of the rural credit sector through branch expansion, informal sector still plays an important role in rural and urban credit. This is because of the transaction costs (both monetary and non-monetary) and more satisfaction that a borrower derives from informal agencies in comparison with formal agencies. Ananth S. Rao and M.N. Dandekar[42] have developed an interest to study as to why the rural sector continues to cling to the money-lenders in spite of concessionary interest and other advantages like technical consultancy services etc. that are available in the formal sector. Transaction cost of formal institutions can be catagorised into monetary & non-monetary costs. The monetary costs relate to the costs paid by way of interest on deposits, borrowings and refinance to provide resources for agricultural credit. The non-monetary costs include the expenses on staff salaries and facilities like office rent, furniture, stationary, travel, telephone communications etc. Rao and Dandekar found that, "non-monetary transaction costs of formal credit institutions are substantial and have an inverse relation with the size of the loan." Although the total monetary and non-monetary transaction cost of the formal sector is lower than the interest cost of the informal sector, the borrower is attracted to the latter because of the simple methods and formalities adopted by the sector. So, the costs incurred by the lending formal agency should try to minimise costs, of lean appraisals, supervisions, technical advice to make recoveries in time, cost on communications (travel & telephone etc.). Monetary costs may be minimised by increasing the spread. The profit making bank/branch should compensate the loss making branch/bank. Moreover, a loss making bank/branch, particularly located in rural area should have to solve the problems of ruralites by supplying raw-materials/inputs, marketing outputs, serving the spares and accessories and guidance in credit utilization. Thus bank's responsibility in rural area is predominant in relation to urban biased banks. If these banks shoulder an extra responsibility a rurally located bank will function viably. But this is not initially considered and emphasised by bureaucrats of public sector banks located in rural area, where the spread is less and cost of transactions are higher.

3.5. Productive Vs Consumption Credit Analysis

Credit for acquiring productive assets is essential for the success of agriculture. Earlier the man used to "earn his bread by the sweat off his brows'[44] he now earns a living by use of capital Any credit which helps to grow agricultural production is called as productive credit. Agricultural credit may increase the production of the current year or may increase future flow of output over a long period. Generally credit for capital purposes imposes no burden if used properly and productively.

Capital requirement may be classified according to the period, purpose, direct and indirect etc. Generally a borrower borrows for productive purpose, through which he proposes or plans to repay the borrowed amount. Lender eagerly comes forward to lend for such productive purposes, because of a guarantee of repayment. Very rarely a borrower, borrows for consumption purposes. However, a borrower may borrow for productive purpose, and can also possibly use the same for consumption items. If a borrower has other productive assets, or a consumption item itself which may be productive either in short-run or in long-run consumption expenditure is also indirectly help to increase the productivity. Satisfaction of basic needs will increase the efficiency *vis-a-vis* productivity.

A productive credit may be borrowed either for short term (ST) or medium term (MT) or long term (LT). According to the All India Rural Credit Review Committee, the S.T. credit is, "a kind of lumpsum accommodation to fill up the gap in outlay which cannot be met from the cultivator's own resources during the non-income period between two harvests".[45] The Action Programme for co-operative credit circulated by the Ministry of Community Development and Co-operative[46] has suggested that the S.T. needs of the cultivator should be determined chiefly with reference to the prevalent scales of production expenditure on different crops. The needs have been classified in the Action Programme under the following five heads:

(i) Cash requirements for production, fixed on per acre basis, cropwise, for rainfed crops, these should ordinarily be within the area. For irrigated crops, these may go up to one-third.

(ii) Amount required per acre for fertilizers, pesticides, seeds etc. up to the qualities recommended by the extension authorities for each crop. (This part of the credit should be disbursed in kind.)

(iii) An amount in cash to take care of the extra labour charges etc. arising from the use of the inputs mentioned in (ii) normally not exceeding about one-half of the amount availed of under (ii).

(iv) A lumpsum in cash, at not more than about ₹ 50 per family (now it should be to the extent of ₹ 200) to meet some part of the maintenance needs of the family.

(v) An additional cash amount equal to 5 per cent of the produce sold by the member through the co-operative during the previous year. This is by way of encouragement to co-operative marketing.

The medium term (MT) credit is given for a period ranging from 15 months to 5 years for the purpose of medium type of investments in farm business or activities. Various purposes recognised by the RBI for which M.T. loans can be advanced by co-operative credit societies are given below:[47]

(a) Reclamation of land.
(b) Bunding and other land improvements.
(c) Preparation of land for orchards and plantations.
(d) Construction, development and maintenance of irrigation sources (wells, pumps etc.).
(e) Purchase of such machinery, implements and transport equipment as are necessary and conducive to agriculture.
(f) Purchase of such live-stock as is necessary or conducive to agriculture.
(g) Construction of farmhouses and cattle sheds etc.
(h) Purchase, construction and maintenance of such equipment as may be needed for carrying on animal husbandry and allied activities jointly undertaken with agriculture.

(i) Other purchases (such as gardening fencing plantation etc.).
(j) Purchase of milk animals.
(k) Purchase of shares of co-operative sugar factories etc.

The Functional Committee on Co-operative Agricultural Credit NCDC has thus classified the purposes for which M.T. loans are needed into two categories:[48] (a) those connected with maintenance or replacement of existing production assets to be called as normal M.T. requirements, (b) those which may be used for financing new investment for improving the productive capacity of the farm to be named as special M.T. loans.

While the long-term (L.T.) credit is given for the period between 5 to 25 years, the purpose of such loans is a long range investment in agriculture business. The L.T. loans are generally given for:

(i) digging and repair of wells, tanks etc.,
(ii) preparation of land for irrigation,
(iii) reclamation, bunding and land improvements,
(iv) construction of farm-houses, cattle sheds and machine sheds,
(v) horticulture,
(vi) purchase of oil engine, electric pump, etc.,
(vii) purchase of tractor and other agricultural heavy machinery,
(viii) purchase of machinery for sugarcane crushing manufacturing of gur and khandsaries,
(ix) purchase of land for consolidation of holdings,
(x) erection of repairing of houses for agricultural purposes,
(xi) purchase, or acquisition of title to agricultural lands by tenants, and
(xii) liquidation of debts etc.

Although the efficient use of any credit is justifiable specially the M.T. and L.T. credit should be used and managed efficiently on a productive foots. The Royal Commission has stated, many years ago that, an efficient management is essential, unless this is assured, no step forward should be taken. It must be remembered that, while the demand for L.T. loans for productive purposes is limited that for money, other purposes are almost insatiable.[49] M.T. and L.T. loans are almost investment loans, because the actual yield of such investments continues for corresponding few years even after repayment. Thus the production credit may be categorised into current expenses on agriculture and investment in agriculture. In underdeveloped economies the percentage borrowings of S.T. credit is high. In India nearly 80 per cent of total borrowing is related to S.T. credits. It means we still need to borrow for current expenses in agriculture. The current capital requirement or variable capital credit leads to gainful results immediately after its application. Whereas the fixed capital credit helps to cumulate its production effects in the long-run.

Duggan and Battles[50] have classified the capital requirement into four kinds:

1. Estate capital — land, permanent improvements.
2. Machinery, farmhouse, equipment, cattle sheds, etc.
3. Operational capital — livestock, fertilizer.
4. Capital for co-operatives for efficient marketing services through their own co-operatives.

S.S.M. Desai[51] classified the productive credit into three categories:

1. Settlement credit–required for new settlements, rehabilitation, construction of farm sheds, farm building etc.
2. Development credit–required for levelling of fields, construction of drainage, digging of wells, irrigation schemes etc., and
3. Equipment credit–required for tractor, pump sets, repairs of machines or maintenance expenses etc.

Thus, agricultural credit issued for current agricultural expenses and capital accumulation in agricultural yield greater agricultural production. Any creditor is interested in issuing such productive credit because of easy repayment possibilities. But, sometimes the credit may not be used for the purpose for which it is taken. In most of such cases credit is used for consumption purposes. This is called as diversion of credit. "The term diversion, therefore, connotes the use of funds (in part or in full) for purposes (desirable or undesirable) other than those for which the loan was originally sanctioned. This in effect means the difference between the total amount borrowed from the bank and the total amount utilised for the approved agricultural purposes."[52] The Programme Evaluation Organisation Reports[53] have also defined 'DR' (Diversion of Credit) on the same lines. Mr. M.L. Bhat [54] has found out certain reasons for such diversion of credit. They are: (i) absence of effective supervision, (ii) inadequate attention to making reliable estimates of cost of the project, (iii) restrictive lending policies which lead to granting loans without fully taking into account the cost of the purpose, (iv) long time gap between sanctioning and disbursement of loans.

Production credit by agriculturists, if properly used, leads to incremental income enabling them to repay the same in early instalments. Such loans are given only after taking into consideration, the repayment potential because it is gradually realised that it is a double edged weapon significantly increasing welfare of human misery, broadening participation of the masses in the political progress or re-enforcing feudalism.[55] While borrowing credit for agricultural purposes, the farmers have to be cautious.

On the other hand, consumption credit is emphasised nowadays as infrastructural base for productive activity. Credit which is borrowed and used for consumption purposes is called consumption credit. Consumption loans are mainly demanded by small and marginal farmers, of course some medium and large landowners also use a part of productive credit for their consumption purposes. However, for them it is easier to adjust the flow of funds with the repayment of loan through their productive capacities either in agriculture or in allied activities. The small and marginal farmers, because of very small land holding, are not in a position to avail of large amount of credit, and their ability to generate incremental production tends to remain very much limited. But their consumption remains the same. Therefore, it becomes inevitable for them to borrow for consumption purposes. Slow during the off season, agriculturists and agricultural labourers do not get any gainful work. During such periods, consumption credit has to be taken from easily accessible agencies. Such credits are mostly issued by non-institutional credit agencies. The reason is that institutional credit agencies will not lend credit to non-creditworthy borrowers, although they may really be in need of borrowed funds. PACS to some extent sanction consumption loans up to ₹ 300 to 500 per family. B. Shivaraman Committee[56] recommended ₹ 650 as annual per family annual consumption credit by commercial banks, even when an inflationary ratio has doubled during the period. It is essential to review the functioning of consumption credit, and the credit to non-creditworthy borrowers. B. Shivaraman Committee recommended to reorganise the PACS before they begin to issue consumption loans. Non-creditworthy credit borrowers, particularly who are rural artisans can get the benefit under various govt. schemes through banking agencies. But the percentage of such borrowers and amount disbursed by the banking agencies is much below one per cent. Credit to consumption purposes is harmful to the bank agency because of the doubtful repayment capabilities of the borrowers. However, some percentage of credit is disbursed as a social commitment of the banking agency. Co-operatives, no doubt are inspired by social welfare and social commitment, by coming together and working together and the commercial banks have also begun to help non-creditworthy borrowers, as social responsibility. In issuing such credit, the capacity of repayment is to be carefully observed. The purposes of consumption loans are generally for (a) medical expenses, (b) educational needs, (c) expenses relating to marriage ceremonies, (d) expenses relating to funerals, births etc., and (e) expenses for religious ceremonies etc. The Shivaraman Committee has clarified these requirements in a logical manner.

John Maynard Keynes has explained that the demand for money comprises of three motives: (a) transaction motive, which is $Lt = f(y)$, is lacking in poor masses, (b) precautionary motives which is $Lp = f(y)$, is again lacking among poor masses *i.e.* non-creditworthy borrowers, and (c) speculative motive, which is determined on $Ls = f(r)$ the rate of interest which has nothing to do with poor masses. Poor people always adjust their day-to-day expenses *i.e.* money required for daily transactions. They earn according to their expenses or *vice-versa*. So, for such purposes, farmers will not borrow consumption loans. But if non-creditworthy borrower farmer, when faces unexpected expenses due to illness, accidents and natural hazards, he has to rush to borrow. And on such occasions it is essential to help him on social and on human grounds. No poor farmer demands money for speculative motives. Thus, consumption loans are meant for unexpected needs of the poor farm population.

B. Shivaraman Committee has clarified the consumption credit needs on the following manner: (i) medical expenses relating to the borrower and the members of his family is a problem in a rural setting. Even where attention is available in a village from a health centre or a charitable dispensary, a farmer is often put to a lot of expenses (apart from the medicines he might have to purchase and requirements of better diet) due to his incapacity to earn his livelihood during the period of illness and recovery. Sometimes, one of the earning members of the family may have to be on attendance, thereby losing one's capacity to earn, (ii) Though free primary education is expected to be available to all citizens, school expenses are often beyond the capacity of a poor man earning his daily bread, (iii) No provision can certainly be made for dowry which has been declared as a social evil. In spite of all the economy one may advocate, there are certain expenses relating to the wedding ceremonies, (iv) Some expenditure is absolutely unavoided on certain occasions, (v) Certain religious ceremonies are so deeply rooted in our culture that they are considered essential by certain section of society.

Majority of agricultural families require consumption loans. But unfortunately most of the institutional agencies are not interested in such credit and if issued the amount remains very small. Moreover, borrowers have to fulfil various formalities to receive such credit. Therefore, agriculturists are compelled to approach non-institutional credit agencies. Consumption credit is essential only because it is infrastructural for participation in productive activities. After fulfilment of consumption needs a person can actively participate in production and production will be efficiently undertaken. Otherwise a 'vicious circle' may operate, keeping both agriculture and agriculturists in a low level equilibrium trap.

The General Report of the Committee of Direction emphasised, "The subsistence needs of the agricultural producer – as distinguished from specific consumption needs connected with marriages, funerals etc., – should be treated as needs which may be legitimately fulfilled, and ought to be effectively fulfilled, by the system of productive finance have recommended. Such needs will automatically be covered if the quantum of crop loan — at so much per acre of the particular crop cultivated — is properly fixed for each area after taking into account all the relevant consideration.[57] The Crop Loan Evaluation Committee[58] of the Bombay State Co-operative Bank, took account of the ineffectiveness of the system so far as small and tenant farmers were concerned. The Committee made a recommendation which broadened the concept and brought about a change in the character of the crop loans. The small farmers have to sustain themselves and their families till the harvest of crops and for this subsistence they require some cash. This cash amount is as essential for growing a crop as any production expenditure. The Committee, therefore pointed out, "as regards the measure of adequate crop finance, it is common ground that all cash outlays needed for purposes of cultivation including labour and material requirements should be covered by it. As to the labour of the cultivating family itself, the tendency has been to exclude its wages or even maintenance expenses from the calculation of cash needs. While some plausible arguments can be produced in support of this practice, it is undeniable that if the marginal and sub-marginal farmers with whom we would be dealing are left without adequate credit for their own maintenance during the cultivation season, they would as surely fall into the hands of money-lenders as if credit were denied to them for the more obvious requirements of seed, fertilizer or hired labour." Consumption (subsistence) credit is a must, therefore should be included in the regulator crop-loan, and other ST loans and MT loans etc.

3.6. Kind Loans *Vs.* Cash Loans

The practice of kind loans has emerged to avoid diversion of credit and to strengthen repayment capacity. Now-a-days agricultural credit is linked with marketing which also aims at reducing incidence of defaults. Credit in kind is also an effective way of avoiding or minimising defaults. All three categories of credit *viz.* ST, MT and LT clarify the role of kind loans. The ST agricultural kind loans generally take the form of supply of seeds, pesticides, fertilizers etc. The MT and LT are mainly hire purchase or secured loans. Hire purchase schemes in respect of agricultural equipment is another example of loan in kind. This scheme is being practised by many credit agencies because surety of repayment. The Central Banking Enquiry Committee (para 100) thought that "the long-term loan .... advanced should be repayable from the margin of profit of the borrower's holding without putting him to the necessity of starving his current financial needs (domestic and occupational) or of borrowing from another source, or of selling his holding to discharge the loan." And, it is obvious that a man who takes advances for long period on personal security takes risks. The risk of default increases with the period for which the loan is made. So, managerial skill to use the credit is emphasised. The MT and LT credit schemes are meant to provide technical service to the agricultural development and infrastructure. In very rare cases MT loans may not be in kind, but indirectly identified and examine the use for which they are borrowed.

The successful operation of kind loan scheme requires direct link between production and service centres by a credit agency. Some credit agencies follow a method of issuing both in kind and in cash. In such a scheme, the borrowing farmer is expected to submit purchase bills for the agricultural inputs, only after which the loan instalment is released. However, under this scheme a farmer may submit a bill paid received by some other farmer and avail of the loan instalment. Some other agencies follow a method of issuing kind loans directly to the farmers. Co-operative banks follow this method. This method has a drawback. Farmers have to accept the fertilizers, seeds, or pesticides which they may not find appropriate to their needs. However, issuing of credit for hire purchase of agricultural equipment is the best example of kind loan. The LDBs issue such credit to the farmers for buying tractors, threshers, pump sets, pipelines for irrigation and for other agricultural implements.

The purpose of the kind loan system is to do away with the need for supervision over the utilisation of credit and thus avoid possible diversion of credit. Thus in kind loan the banker's interest is protected because it ensures the recovery of the loans. Moreover, a banker has to serve according to the rules and regulations in existence. Therefore, each system has both merits and demerits. It all depends upon the borrowers' character — how they use the credit, the purpose for which they use the credit and the productivity which they create from the credit. Unless a kind of moral responsibility is created among the borrowers, it is very difficult to get a safe productive system of credit. Our farmers have to face a number of economic exigencies, which compel them to divert the credit. It, however, remains a fact that in a sound credit system, both elements of credit, kind loans and cash loans are essential.

The decisions, whether to issue credit either in cash or in kind should be left to the bankers who may take the decision according to the specific position of the borrowing farmers. The progressive farmers may repay the loan even when they divert the credit for other purposes, because they have the ability to follow the repayment schedules. In the case of such farmers, full or partial kind loans should not be made obligatory. However, it is always better to issue some portion of loan as kind loan and remaining in cash. The credit to small and marginal farmers should be in kind. But there is need to specify the loans to be paid in kind and the loans to be paid in cash. For example, S.T. credit which is meant for seeds, fertilizers, irrigation, minor equipments, and machineries, pesticides and herbicides and other minor expenses may be issued in kind. And other MT and LT credit should be issued in kind either directly or indirectly. And in the case of such loans, it is necessary to create linkages with various agencies who produce or supply agricultural inputs. It is in this respect that proper management becomes essential. If such efficient management is present risk in supplying credit may automatically be minimised. Mr. G. Herald has remarked, "how nice it would be if when a farmer comes to my bank, I would stick a management thermometer in his mouth and get a reading which could tell me that he had the skill and knowledge to handle a \$20,000 to \$50,000 enterprise effectively."[59] Royal Commission on Agriculture also emphasised the efficient management.[60] Normally banking agency confines its management to effective disbursement and recovery of the loans. They seem to be indifferent about the impact and the effect that their lending creates in the rural setting.

3.7. Principles of Micro and Macro Financing to Agriculture

Micro financing to agriculture may be defined as finance issued to an individual farmer for improvement of his agricultural practices leading to increased agricultural production. Individual finance or micro-finance may be issued in accordance with the assets of individual borrower. Such finance is supposed to help the borrower in the acquisition of additional assets in future, *i.e.* purchase of land, investment on land improvements, irrigation, livestock, farmhouse construction, implements etc. In a poor country, land is the only asset which can be used as pledge for agricultural finance, "In a comparatively poor country ..... where there is very little movable property apart from cattle, implements and seed .... land is not merely the best but often the only security that can be pledged by a borrower."[61] In India credit facilities have been provided to farmers on the security of land well from 1863 (Sinha, 1927).

Macro finance may be defined as financial policy of the state for agricultural development. Micro-finance has a direct impact on the individual borrower, while macro-finance has collective impact on the economy as a whole. State's policies are guidelines for microlending procedures etc. Macro-financing depends upon the position of agriculture in the total economy of the State. The priorities of State's economic policy may clarify the state's attitude towards agricultural sector. A predominantly agricultural economy should concentrate on agricultural financing. Provision of adequate and appropriate finance to all sectors of the economy is also called as macro financing policy. Poor performance of a sector may be the cause of inadequate provision of finance to that sector. Development has a directive push through credit. This is more so in case of rural development which can be made possible by introducing finances for agricultural purposes. It need not be emphasised that agricultural development crucially depends on appropriate and adequate credit facilities. Macro-finance emphasises the provision of credit which facilitates the adoption of modern technology by the farmers. On the other hand, micro-finance depends on individual decisions and attitudes of the borrowers, *i.e.*, When to borrow? How much to borrow? From whom to borrow? For what to borrow? How to use the credit? How to repay the credit etc. Credit is one of the adjustable factors in agriculture (Redman 1971) which is left with the decision-makers. Lending by institutions is best governed by a set of rules and procedures of macro-financing policies, which should often be flexible. Government must assist development of the financial institutions catering credit to the individual farmers by taking shares, providing guarantees providing subsidies, contributing to special bad debt, reserve funds, providing grants helping to set credit relief funds etc. Another benefit of macro-financing policy is that it implies state interference in day-to-day working of financial institutions. It is the responsibility of the Govt. to provide cheap, safe, accessible and productive credit to the needy farmers but not necessary by direct provision. Macro policy for agricultural financing may be direct or indirect. Direct benefits may be grouped into three: (a) primary benefits which include government-contribution for shares, subsidies, contribution to bad debt funds, grants, relief funds, concessions etc., (b) secondary benefits include, provision of guarantees, differential interest rates, and priority to agriculture sector etc., (c) tertiary benefits comprise facilities to help the agencies who help in agricultural financing, guidelines for proper operation of agricultural finance, provision of infrastructure, creation of credit potentialities, bio-engineering, institutional support for transportation etc.

The macro-agricultural financing policy should have following objectives (Sharma 1980): (i) To improve the miserable low standard of living of the agriculturists by making agriculture a "business rather than way of life." (ii) To help augment agricultural production and consequently strengthen the farm economy, (ii) Encourage the agriculturists to adopt new agricultural technology, (iv) To provide cheap credit both to those who have means to offer security as well as to those who are willing and capable of producing more through added inputs and better farm management ensuring easy recovery, (v) Assistance in the development of resourcefulness among big, medium and small farmers alike, (vi) Proper supervision of the use of credit, (vii) Provision of both production and consumption credit to farmers so that they are freed from the clutches of the moneylenders. (vii) Timely, adequate and cheap supply of credit to the farmers, (ix) Inculcate thrift and saving among the farmers through better use of capital.

These principles are general guidelines for micro-financing agencies who have direct contact with agriculturists. But in certain circumstances it is difficult to make them operative due to certain gaps in the functioning of the credit agencies. S. Nakkiran[62] has given, adequacy, proximity, reasonable rate of interest, supervision and self-management as cannons of good credit for agriculture. Rural Credit Survey Committee has also stated certain requirements of effective institutional credit system for rural India.[63]

Micro-financing for agriculture is undertaken by various agencies. Micro-financing has to look into the economical, technical and financial feasibility of agricultural financing. Emphasis on such feasibility factors by individual agencies is necessary to avoid the risk in micro-lending. Credit agencies have to provide credit for the genuine needs of agriculturists and such credit should be cheap, safe, accessible and adequate. To avoid the problems like diversion of credit and delay in repayment, linking of credit with marketing at the micro-level needs to be adopted. Traditionally, credit agencies base their credit appraisal on,

(i) the purpose of the loan,
(ii) the standing and character of the borrowers,
(iii) his repaying capacities and his past repayment performance,
(iv) the tangible/collateral security, and
(v) the share-holding in the lending society.

These are the criteria used for determining individual credit limit. In Maharashtra, under the crop loan system, banks while fixing up the credit limit of the co-operative societies, take into account the managerial efficiency as reflected in repayment of loans, arrangements for supervision of the use of credit, facilities for marketing, and ability of the society for marketing, controlling the disposal of the production of the members.[64] Credit agencies classify credit disbursement according to period, purpose, security and socio-economic importance etc. which include repaying capacities, production potentialities, gestation period, and incremental income of the borrowers. Mr. M. Luis Tardy,[65] an authority on agricultural credit has pointed out that the following are the important criteria of sound agricultural credit:

(a) It should be granted for a sufficiently long period commensurate with the length of the operation which it is designed to facilitate.

(b) It should be granted at a low rate of interest.

(c) It should be adequately secured in order, more particularly, to avoid any abuse of credit facilities, but the security should not necessarily be material.

(d) The security should, if necessary, be in the form of a personal credit secured mainly by the borrower's socio-moral standing and farming ability.

(e) It should be related to the average yield and capacity for repayment of the farms, particularly during periods of economic depression.

(f) It (credit appraisal) should be placed in the hands of institutions, the directors of which have received special training and have actual banking experience.

Besides this, a banking agency, which provides credit to agriculturists must have direct contact with them. The timely and adequate supply of credit helps the agriculturists to boost their agricultural production. There is" an old adage which says, "late credit is no credit," because farmers have to adjust according to changing climatic conditions. Therefore, day-to-day technical guidance to farmers should be provided by banks. The cost of credit should be minimum. Disbursement of credit and repayment of loans should have in suitable instalments. The kind components of loans should be provided well in time. Irrigated land-holders have greater potentiality to borrow credit. The intensity of inputs should be observed through experts from the credit agencies. Adequate use of credit increases the income substantially. Even at the prevailing state of the technology and at the current level of technology there exists a large potential market for credit.[66] Successful functioning of the agricultural finance depends upon the above factors. However, the real success depends upon the proper administration of both lender's and borrower's activities. According to F.A.O., "The administration of agricultural credit must be a part of a group of technical and humanitarian activities in such a way that it is an integrating part of coherent whole."[67] Therefore, the functional and structural adoption of lending operation towards agriculture should be efficient, active and well prepared to sustain increasing volume of finance to agricultural sector. Various projects and areas, which have greater potentiality for institutional finance should be created by the Govt. Micro-level research and investigation will certainly justify the need for the institutional credit. "Any programme of agricultural finance, in addition to micro-economic approach, must also be based on a macro-economic analysis and unless the inter-sectoral adjustments in the light of the general framework are made, the maximisation of common good may not be achieved. It is, therefore, necessary to give due weightage to other sectors of the economy too, because agriculture is the most important sector of the economy and a very large share of the population depends on it. This sector automatically should be given greater importance in any scheme of institutional finance and the advanced districts/ tehsil/regions have the first claim."[68]

3.8. Three 'RS' in Agricultural Finance

Agricultural finance has two aspects, *i.e.* acquisition of loans and the maximum and efficient utilisation of loans in farm activities. First aspect is institutional business while the other is borrower's business. Both entrepreneurs, the bankers and farmers try to maximise their satisfaction in farm finance activities. Institutional entrepreneur has to bear risk and uncertainty regarding repayment of loans; while the farm entrepreneur has to know the marginal productivity of the loan on his farm for its rational and optimal use and through which he has to learn its jurisdiction of utilisation; so that the returns to the fixed farm resources are maximised. Other incentives remaining the same, large and irrigated landholding strengthen the intention to borrow. Any kind of technological change too, increases the intention to borrow. Finance helps to change technological traditions with reorganisation of production plans in agricultural practices. Thus agricultural finance should lead to greater on the borrowed investment, which again will strengthen the farm assets and repaying capacity of a farmer.

Aaron G. Nelson and William G. Murray[69] and S.S. Johl and C.V. Moore,[70] emphasise considerations of returns, repayment capacity and risk-bearing ability, which are referred to as the three '₹' of agricultural credit. These terms are in a sense indicator of three 'Cs' of agricultural credit *i.e.* character (risk of returns), capacity (repayment) and capital (risk bearing).

First, it is very important to analyse the additional returns *vis- a-vis* the additional cost in utilising borrowed funds. This is a problem of credit management within the broad framework of credit management and involves maximisation of returns to the fixed farm resources (including the borrowed capital resources). It is basically related to the question of what to produce, how much to produce and how to produce, when to sell and where to sell. Important points to be remembered in this analysis are:

(i) "Estimates of returns should be made on the basis of total resources including the borrowed funds.

(ii) Estimates of returns and costs should be made at the margin and not an average basis.

(iii) Not only must be marginal cost equal to marginal revenue principle kept in view, while deciding upon the amount of credit, but law of equi-marginal returns must be fully observed.

(iv) The level of other resources (land and labour) should also be considered before deciding upon the amount of working capital to be used. This means that the possibilities of enhancing the level of the most important resources limiting farm production should also be examined carefully.

(v) Due care has to be taken to ensure that more than the required amount of money is not advanced. At the same time, inadequate amount of funds would not serve any useful purpose. Funds should, therefore, be advanced neither inadequately nor excessively but just the right amount that can be profitably used.

(vi) Money needed for consumption purposes should also be considered for their marginal value to the farm family satisfaction against the marginal productivity of the production loans."[71]

Secondly, repayment has two approaches: (a) conventional approach with emphasis on credit limit, and (b) modern approach, which is based on production plans. The modern approach considers the question whether the borrower will have sufficient repayment capacity and mortgage? A loan may be profitable, but the farmer still may not be able to meet the repayments as they come due. Repayment capacity may be assessed with following methods:[72]

(a) Marketable surplus method—which has been computed by taking into account the previous stocks plus net farm produce in the year minus consumption requirement till the next harvest. The balance if any, is the marketable surplus in that particular year and presumably determines the repayment capacity of the borrower at the current prices of the product.

(b) Liquidity Method — which measure the repayment capacity through excess of receipts over the payments in cash, and

(c) Liquidity and marketable surplus method which emphasise the repayment capacity measured by the excess of income over expenditure. This may be symbolically given as,[73]

$$RC = Y - C$$

Where, RC = Repaying capacity,

Y = Gross income - farm expenses met from owned funds + non-farm income.

C = Consumption expenditure.

Both income and expenditure items are listed below:

Income	*Expenditure*
(i) Previous balance (cash and kind)	(i) Household expenses (cash and kind)
(ii) Net farm product	(ii) Farm expenses paid (cash and kind)

(iii) Borrowings	(iii) Any amount paid to creditors other than co-operatives.
(iv) Cash and kind receipts cultivation.	(iv) Expenses on repairs and from sources other than maintenance of assets.
(v) Realisation of loans interest	(v) Requirement of households.
(vi) Money from disposal capital assets.	(vi) Reserve for contingency and liquidity.
(vii) Any other receipts.	

The repaying capacity may be strengthened by the following measures:

1. Through increasing equity.
2. Removing the imbalance in resource availability.
3. Adjusting the time period of loan requirements.
4. Improving input efficiency through resource use planning.
5. Adjustment in the type of loan.
6. Introduction of new and more profitable enterprises and adopting improved technology.
7. Proper marketing of farm produce.
8. Improving the management skill of the cultivators.[74] Further Johl and Moore have given various alternative repayment plans, (a) lumpsum repayment plan, (b) amortised even repayment plan, (c) amortised decreasing repayment plan, and (d) variable or quasi-variable repayment plan,[75] etc.

Thirdly, risk bearing has two types of aspects, one, borrower's unexpected losses, and, two, lender's unexpected losses.; Lender's risk is protected by mortgage of borrower's-assets, while borrower's risk, if borne by him, will not be covered. Therefore, the borrower's risk bearing ability may be strengthened through increasing his willingness to save, strengthening the will to borrow in bad times, to acquire equity and net worth and to create ability to adjust in adverse conditions. But the risk remains with the borrower. At times of unexpected difficulties his only way out is to find out adjustment plans. To avoid this kind of risk, it would be worthwhile to assess at the time of lending, whether the farmer has the ability to carry the risk and uncertainty involved in using credit supplied by credit institutions. The technical feasibility of loan project should be observed with economic, organisational and managerial skills of the credit users. NABARD has given the guidance to use the checklist for considering and control of crop loans. (See Appendix-1). More distinctly, risk and repayment capacities are determined by the factors either directly or indirectly involved in the farm finance.

$$G = J(T)^{n76}$$

Where,

G = risk in terms of percentage of investment.

T = repaying capacity

Jn = are constants which depend upon farm situations.

It is clear from the above equation that, repaying capacity depends upon farm situations and farmer's credit-worthiness. Sometimes adoption of new technology through credit strengthens the risk bearing capacity.

APPENDIX NO. 1

Nabard's Checklist for Considering Sanction and Control of Crop Loans

1. *Know the villages through:*
   - (i) Land: type of soil.
   - (ii) Trends of rainfall during the 3 years if available.
   - (iii) Modes of Irrigation,
   - (iv) Extent of land under each type of irrigation.
   - (v) Types of crops grown in each season.
   - (vi) Average yields obtaining in the village.
   - (vii) Natural calamities that occurred in the village in the recent past and the extent of damage.
   - (viii) No. of electric motors/diesel engines, tractors, power tillers.
   - (ix) No. of progressive farmers with names, name of seed growers, if any.
2. *Know the applicant through interview and verification:*
   - (i) Name and address and father's name.

(ii) Members of the family with names and ages.

(iii) Nature and extent of holding: (a) owned (b) leased — if leased type of lease — registered/oral/share cropping.

(iv) Cropping pattern adopted earlier.

(v) Nature of irrigation facility available.

(vi) Whether the proposed cropping pattern is consistent with irrigation facility available on the farm.

(vii) Labour — from within the family, outside labour. How many needed, availability and cost.

(viii) Existing position of liabilities, names of institution/ individual account, due to be repaid by security offered.

(ix) Whether the applicant is also a money-lender.

(x) Quantum of loan sought.

(xi) Is it consistent with the recommended seal finance for the crop proposed?

(xii) If there is any variation, find out the reasons.

(xiii) Is there any seed corporation or other agency purchasing the produce at the end of the season?

(xiv) Annual family expenses.

3. *Technical Aspects:*

(i) Varieties of crops and practices obtaining and proposed to be adopted.

(ii) Soil and climatic conditions.

(iii) Plant protection measures generally adopted *vis-a-vis* those that become necessary.

4. *Commercial Aspects:*

(a) (i) Availability of inputs locally or at a nearby place.

(ii) Are the prices of inputs reasonable?

(iii) Is it possible to arrange for supply of inputs in kind from these agencies and the reliability of these agencies for supply on time.

(b) Marketing of produce:

(i) Commercial crops, linkage with commodity boards wherever they are available,

(ii) Cereals crops: procurement agencies.

3.9. Principles of Supervised Credits

The financial system of supervised credit is an outcome of the need for avoiding the diversion of credit and to strengthen the repayment capacities of the borrowing farmers. Sometimes it is assumed that lenders try to strengthen their own risk bearing capacities by supervising utilisation of their loans. However, supervised credit presupposes technical guidance to the borrowers. This guidance should begin with pre-lending survey of credit requirement to the final repayment of loans. At every stage, the technical experts from the credit agency should guide the farmers in their farming activities. Supervised credit is nothing but educating the farmers in his farm business. Various agricultural credit agencies follow and favour this method of credit disbursement. Commercial banks sanction their agricultural credit through Agricultural Department of the bank. In other cases, bank inspectors supervise the credit. Some banks have recovery officers. In co-operative movement to the supervised credit system has been in practice for a long time.[77] However, the co-operative movement in India is faced with an extremely difficult and massive task, on a huge scale among a people with no training in business or self-help, that is why there was only qualified success.[78] Very recently the RBI has appointed a committee under the chairmanship of Dr. Khushro to evaluate the working of co-operative credit societies and measures to strengthen the rural banking business in India.

S.C. Jain[79] has defined the supervised credit as a particular system of credit, wherein management of loan remains in the hands of the lenders, which co-ordinates credit provision with extension services or farm plans and aim at effective supervision of loan utilisation. The supervised credit system strengthens the creditworthiness of the borrowing farmers. Though the system adds to the cost of credit, it is necessary in farm finance because it aims at:

(a) training farmers for the adoption of improved farm practices.
(b) making available adequate credit to these farmers on production capacity basis determined by a farm plan.

(c) helping farmers in the purchase of inputs like seeds, fertilizers, implements, pesticides etc. at reasonable prices.
(d) promoting the development of agro-based industries and their subsidiary and supplementary enterprises which may add to farmers agricultural abilities.

The development of a detailed system of supervised individual credit has significance not only for financial operations but also for the entire process and development planning. Therefore, all banking agencies should help in the procedure and administration of supervision. A beginning has been made in Maharashtra in two *directions:* (a) in the joint planning and implementation of annual targets by co-operative department and co-operative banks, (b) in the attempts made to coordinate fully the work of the co-operative central banks and cooperative development banks.[80] But this is at macro-level. On a macrolevel the supervision at institutional level has been emphasised since Maclagan Committee Report till today. Particularly co-operative hierarchy emphasises supervision on its lower level institutions. Moreover, separate supervisory unions are also formed to look into the functioning of PACS. It was in 1915 that the guaranteeing unions were organised for PACS situated with the radius of about 5 miles to serve as a liaison between the primaries and the provincial cooperative bank. They performed the function of supervision and also furnished guarantee to the financing agency for advances made to societies within their area.[81] Then supervisory unions were formed in 1922 at taluka places. Various modifications were then formulated in the organisation of such supervisory unions in Maharashtra.

The supervision of credit has two aspects: (a) internal (b) external. Internal supervision is a work being carried out by a lending agency. That is, it should concentrate on the proper utilisation of credit borrowed by a farmer. And external supervision is, supervision of upper agency on lower agency. Such supervision should be distinctly different and connote much more than routine inspection. Co-operative supervisory unions, were assigned to supervise, "the duty of instructing the members in co-operative principles and propagation of the movement by the organisation of new societies."[82] At present such type of macro-level supervision and planning are being operated through Lead Bank Scheme. The role of Lead Bank Scheme is immense, as the co-operative department has brought the supervision for educating and motivating the rural people toward co-operative society. Other than co-operatives, there is no supervisory agency to supervise over the lending agencies which lend agricultural credit. In this sense Lead Bank Scheme is significant, because it prepares an annual plan of action and annual credit plan. Thus on an agency level, supervision will come automatically as an administrative need. But the supervision on credit management at micro-level should be emphasised, even when a lending agency verifies the repayment schedule and the economics of loan, so far lent to a farmer. The agricultural department of commercial banks, with its experts in agricultural science, try to supervise the credit lent for agricultural purposes, while a District Co-operative Bank declares the loan limits to each type of credit *i.e.* ST and MT which are being lent through PACS, wherein economics of agricultural loan is identified with regional characteristics and features, prevailing in a district area. The supervision at micro-level credit utilisation is essential, because both lender and borrower will, get the benefits of such supervision. However, supervision in the sense should not be like bossing; it should educate the farmers in farm business according to the science of cultivation. Moreover, a social and personal relations will strengthen the moral and psychological feeling towards development and growth. A lending agency should treat the borrower as a member and their family.

Thus, supervised credit aims at better impact of credit on agricultural business, which simultaneously results into improving the living conditions of the farming community. Dario B. Brossard[83] has pointed out that, "the system of supervised credit is not an ordinary banking credit system, since it depends, mainly upon education work of agricultural officers to plan and carry out his work and to market his produce, and upon home economic officers (usually women) assisting the farmer's wife in household affairs. In fact this system of credit depends basically on the influence excercised by the field staff over the farmer, his family and the rural community in which they live. They are primarily responsible for its success and failure." As supervision and guidance are excercised over the borrower both as a farmer and as a household, the supervisory staff should be efficient and social, capable of guessing the genuineness of farmer's need. In the initial phase of supervised credit programme, more emphasis should be placed on economic aspects, helpful in increasing farmer's income, which will produce more receptive attitude and a favourable basis for social improvements. To achieve this objective most of the credit agencies choose to lend for cash crops (*e.g.* crop loan to sugarcane, cotton, tobacco etc.) or other agricultural produce, which is generally produced for the market purpose *(e.g.* onion, potatoes, turmeric, chilies etc.).

A credit agency which prefers lending through supervision emphasises pre-lending survey of farmers. In such surveys, mostly the feasibility factors of (supervised) credit implementation are found out without emphasising security or pledge. The type of security required by a supervised credit programme must be within the actual or potential possibility of the farmers and must be complemented by supervision and technical guidance. The use of funds is guided rather than controlled. However, pre-lending surveys are very significant, because supervised credit programme offers two services *i.e.* credit and extension (education) to farmers. As the system aims at helping the farmers through better farming and improved living conditions of a farmer's family it should involve a careful pre-lending survey by an agri-expert of the lending agency. The repayment schedule must be carefully arranged and the money for the purpose must come from the increased cash income derived from the implementation of the farming plan. It is also essential to provide additional funds for raising the standard of living as well as for motivating additional savings and capital investment. Therefore, planning and supervisory process are very crucial in this system of lending. In underdeveloped countries this type of credit system will work effectively provided the supervisory staff works with the sense of belongingness towards the borrower families. The system is very useful, specially, for the improvement of economic conditions of small and marginal farmers. However, in practice it is only the rich farmers who show eagerness to get benefits of this scheme, and credit agencies also show greater interest in their well-being.

In India, most of the agricultural schemes, specially meant for small and medium farmers, in operation benefit mainly the rich farmers. This has been one of the common findings of a series of researches into green revolution.

A group of F.A.O. experts and field specialists in supervised agricultural credit met in Rome, with a view to exchanging ideas and formulating a policy for future F.A.O. work. The following are the guidelines of supervised credit which emerged in their deliberations:[84]

(i) The scheme of supervised credit should concentrate on viable small and medium farmers with a view to efficient and effective utilisation of credit.
(ii) Supervised credit should be effectively linked with cooperative credit, marketing, land settlement and land reforms.
(iii) The implementation of the supervised credit should be based on careful study of the area and beneficiaries and with the support of local leadership.
(iv) In the initial stages, the supervised credit scheme should go in mainly for income increasing economic areas (cash crops) which will sustain the future growth of the scheme.
(v) There should be a continuous programme of educating and training local leadership in the essential of supervised credit and its need and importance.
(vi) As far as possible, avoiding the creation of new administrative machinery, the use of existing co-operative credit and extension services may be maximised.
(vii) As far as possible, scheme of supervised credit should be implemented through co-operatives only. This will keep the costs down and will get local response more easily.
(viii) Pilot projects combining supervised credit with co-operative (credit, marketing, farm supplies) and agricultural extension senders may well provide important lessons for creating or expanding a nation-wide system of agricultural cooperatives and credit.

3.10. Principle of Crop Loan

Agricultural credit is a complex problem; since late fifties, there has been an increasing realisation of the complexity of the problem, although it is a vital factor responsible for integrated rural development. The whole problem of agricultural credit was therefore, envisaged with three important ingredients:[85]

1. It was vitally held that, "the co-operative framework, because of its democratic character and the scope it offers for individual initiative, provides the best means of placing agricultural credit on a sound footing, and also that the Govt. concerned must assume major (or full) responsibility for provision of funds, organisational development and supervision of the movement."
2. A second feature was the "realisation of the intimate relationship between agricultural credit and marketing of agricultural produce, and of the need for a comprehensive and integrated approach to these questions. Underlining this realisation is the fact that an integrated system can facilitate supervision of the use of credit as well as its repayment and can better withstand the competition of private money-lenders and traders."
3. A third and indeed an 'important feature was the awareness of the fact that agricultural credit based on the productive capacity of the borrower (coupled with judicious supervision of credit) is feasible and ought to replace credit based on the security of immovable property.

The third ingredient of new approach is translated into crop loan. This new system had in a way its genesis in the recommendation of the committee of Direction of A.I.R.C.S.C. The system was described as, "(i) in which production is the main purpose of the arrangements for finance; (ii) ST loans are given on the basis that, a crop is anticipated; (iii) the loans are related in amount to the estimated outlay on raising a particular crop; and (iv) the recoveries are made, as and when the crop is sold, from the proceeds of the sale.[86] The concept thus evolved out of experience over a number of years. The system has come up as a device of change in agricultural finance. The major shift was from the asset worthiness to the production-worthiness of the borrower, which is the major aim of our agricultural policy for four decades. Any rapid growth in short-run requires a rapid and radical change in the character of agricultural technology both in bio-technology and mechanical technology which reflected in the use of H.Y.V. of seeds, intensive use of fertilizers, plant protection measures, use of tractor, thresher, harvester etc. The new technology is highly productive, but at the same time more costly and unless proper credit availability in conduction with careful extension advice and other necessary institutional infrastructure are provided to the large majority of cultivators, no substantial achievement can be expected. Agricultural credit in terms of crop loan is a viable source and is meant for meeting costs of some of these critical costly inputs apart from providing sustenance to the farm family during the period preceding the harvest.[87]

Crop loan system is a rational way of financing agriculture, especially in case of small and marginal farmers, who have no assets to pledge but who need the credit for a short period. As the quality of loan depends upon the area of cultivation, large farmers get greater amounts of loan. However, the crop loan provides special opportunity to small and marginal farmers in comparison with other credit facilities. It has been generally maintained that the tenant cultivators, share croppers, small and marginal farmers and agricultural labourers do not get adequate share of credit because of the security oriented loaning system, tardy and slow implementation of land reforms, absence of ownership rights, non-availability of small farmers and dominance of large and medium farmers over the financial system.[88] The commercial banks are reluctant to issue credit to small and marginal farmers, while co-operative are governed by mainly rich and medium farmers. The crop loan first emerged as a device to take co-operative credit, a step beyond the stage where the credit of a cultivator whether explicitly related to the value of owned land not depended larger on his real assets. Crop loan provides sufficient fulfilment of farmers credit needs in comparison with other credit facilities. Every credit need of farmers should sufficiently be fulfilled, otherwise, a very little credit, as pointed out by Professor Laurent (quoted with approval by M.D. Andriment) that, "is not the creator, but simply the mover of capitals.[89] So, crop loan creates some things, adds to the total original assets and is held responsible to the prosperity of farmers.

The evolution of crop loan, goes much back before the initial period of co-operative movement. The first efforts to find out a suitable organisation for providing agricultural credit were made towards the turn of 19th Century, when Mr. Nicholson was deputed by the Government of Madras to study the land bank system in Europe to recommend a suitable system for financing Indian agriculture. Mr. Nicholson reported "Find Raiffeisen," on village to one society and one society to each village. This should be a model for agricultural development through co-operative structure in particular and rural development in general. The inception of co-operative movement was an outcome of Deccan riots. The initial thrust of the co-operative movement was to do away with the situations prevailing due to non-institutional indebtedness and drought conditions during 1870-1875. During 1927-28 S.G. Deodhar, Senior Inspector, Baramati suggested certain norms for crop loan, and during 1930 the crop loan system was introduced locally. Subsequently, the Bansali Mehta Committee, 1938 and Bombay Agricultural Debt and Relief (BARD) Act, 1939, emphasised the need for an institutional agency which will stand as an alternative to money-lenders and suggested Agricultural Credit Corporation. As early as 1950,[90] the RBI had emphasised the need for linking agricultural credit to farm productivity instead of the property owned by the farmer. Later a systematic study was conducted by All India Rural Credit Survey Committee in 1951, and it recommended the introduction of crop loan system. It should, however, be noted that the idea of having some kind of national apex institution for financing agriculture owes its germination to the agricultural credit Deptt. of RBI, which in the subsequent period assumed various forms like ARC, ARDC and finally in the year 1982 crystallised into NABARD, which today initiates the short-term, medium-term and long-term credit to agriculture and rural development. Crop loan is a short-term credit, which is also called as production credit, being issued both by co-operative agencies and commercial banks today. The system was put into operation in 1950. Five Years later a Committee under Chairmanship of D.G. Karve was appointed to evolve the working of the system, to devise further measures for the application of the system more efficiently in the whole of the state and to give general directions for the expansion of credit for production through co-operative organisation. The Committee suggested: (a) crop loan should be related to size of farming unit and should cover maintenance expenditure splitted in cash and kind, (b) crop loan should be recovered out of sale of produce. Later the Standing Advisory Committee, 1963, criticises the central co-operative banks, which had exhibited a tendency to raise the cash components of the crop loan year after year; thus encouraging growers to lift the cash components to the full extent and not touch the kind component. Secondly there should be a season in advances and recoveries. Thus the crop loan system sought to transform the situation in two directions: (i) by shifting the emphasis from real property to the crop as security it brought even pure tenants as potential borrowers and, (ii) by relating the size of loan to the requirement of business emphasised on productive purposes.

The crop loan (working capital) requirements of agriculturists depend on the area of the land cultivated, type of land,' the nature of crops grown, the level of cultivation, whether improved practices of cultivation have been adopted etc.[91] The system indeed necessitated a change in the concept of credit-worthiness of a cultivator. Any farmer who had the capacity to repay a loan taken for short-term farming operations through the sale proceeds of his crop, irrespective of whether he was an owner cultivator or a tenant cultivator was deemed to be credit-worthy under the scheme [92] The scheme has special features, which are mentioned below:

(a) It is productive and emphasizes proper utilisation of the credit.
(b) The term of repayment is short and based on the anticipation of the crop.
(c) The amount of loan is linked to the area of crop.
(d) The amount of loan is related to and differs from crop to crop.
(e) The initial cost of cultivating the crop is borne by crop grower at least up to first three months.

(f) This type of credit is mostly linked to markets or processing units for effecting recoveries out of sale proceeds of the crop raised with the loans. In the area where cash crops are grown and where most of the farmers belong to the cooperative marketing or processing units, the crop loan scheme tend to work more successfully. It is exactly for this reason that PACS have succeeded in agricultural credit more than commercial banks.

Gadgil Committee has explained the features of crop loan as:[93]

1. The primary credit society should try to finance all the short-term needs of its members and also, subject to certain limitations, their intermediate term needs.
2. In a co-operative society the credit-worthiness of a member should be assessed on the basis of his repaying capacity. (This is to be based on the amount of total output and not on the value of assets.)
3. The security for advances should ordinarily be personal. But the society should have a statutory charge on the crop as an additional security for all its seasonal finance, the willful breach of which should be made a criminal offence. Mortgage security may be justified when the size and the period of the loan require it, it should be only collateral.
4. The delay in clearing loan applications should be minimised.
5. Loans should be advanced only as and when they are actually required.
6. Regular repayment of loans should be insisted upon.

The same committee has explained some characteristics of crop loan as under:

(a) It was a production oriented finance.
(b) It was on the basis of a crop and not on the basis of title.
(c) It had to be proportionate to the estimated outlay on raising the crop.
(d) The recovery should be affected as and when the crop was sold from the proceeds of the sale.

(e) It should provide for as large a portion of the total credit as possible in kind *i.e.* in the forms of seeds, fertilizers, manures, etc.

The merits of crop loan system may be explained as under:

(i) Assured repayment is possible.
(ii) The credit may be utilised for which it is borrowed.
(iii) The system provides both kind and cash loans.
(iv) The system introduces the issuing through instalments.
(v) There is a effective linkages between credit and marketing.
(vi) An adequate finance depending on crops will be made available through this system.

The demerits of the system may be as under:

(i) It becomes very difficult to identify the need of borrowers.
(ii) Sometimes, somebody neglect the kind loans.
(iii) The System does not touch the uneconomic-farmers.
(iv) There is also the problem of consumption loans.
(v) The whole system is useful only to commercial crops, and less effective to subsistence agriculture.

Even the rules and regulations as well as procedures of crop loan differ from region to region or from state to state. This is only because of geographical dissimilarities and imbalances in the growth of co-operative movement. Moreover, it is also difficult to determine the scales and components of the credit system in a general form. The taluka area is the most appropriate unit for the estimation of cropping pattern-wise production credit. In Maharashtra under the crop loan system the banks, while fixing up the credit limit of the PACS, depend upon the managerial efficiency (as reflected in repayment of loans), supervision, marketing and ability of the society to control the disposal of the members and the individual criteria of credit limits are determined through the purpose of loan, character of borrower, his repaying capacity, the security and the number of shares he has taken etc.[94]

W.C. Shrishrimal,[95] however, maintained that, "the system as it is defined today can therefore, be said to have a limited and narrow concept. Because of its relation to the crop requirement, the movement is incapable of meeting the major needs of small farmers, for example, if the budget of two agricultural families consisting of 5 persons are taken on a hypothetical basis, it will be seen that the total family budget of a farmer having an irrigated cash crop like cane, the share of co-operative finances comes to nearly 70 to 75 per cent, whereas in the case of the other, growing food crops and cereals the share comes to about 20 to 30 per cent.

This can be illustrated from the following example. A farmer having a cash crop of 3 acres is eligible to get an average ₹ 3600 as crop finance. If on a hypothetical basis his family expenses are taken at ₹ 2000, the total family budget comes to ₹ 5000. Here the share of co-operative finance in his total family budget is nearly 70 per cent. As against this in the case of a farmer who has about 10 acres of land under food crops, even at the liberal-scale he would be eligible for a finance of ₹ 500 and taking his family expenditure to be ₹ 1500 making a total of ₹ 2000 the share of co-operative finance in his total family budget comes to 25 per cent. This clearly brings out the fact that the crop loan system cannot do much in ameliorating the economic position of a small farmer and the grower of non-cash crops.

However, the system provides an opportunity to introduce modern technique of agriculture. The system has specially benefited the medium farmers. The event may be described as a fundamental shift in Indian agricultural production from 3 per cent per annum growth between 1951-65 to about 5.5 per cent per annum between 1966-1971.[96] Small farmers obtain more ST (crop loan) credit plan than long-term.[97] The HYV has modest impact on allotment of credit agencies. Even though the borrower has a fear of repayment within 15 months, there is always possibility of crop loan being used for consumption purposes. But the borrowers adjust with the repayment through other activities or transactions. Thus the demand for credit and repayment depends upon the adoption of new technology in farm business either by small and medium or by a large farmer.

In general only slow progress can be achieved by crop loan process. Otto Schiller has rightly remarked the fact that, "In various developing countries, however, there is an urgent need to achieve a rapid improvement of agricultural techniques and an increase in agricultural production. For this purpose, it is necessary to act more energetically and more systematically than is the case with the ordinary crop loans, which may or may not be accepted by the cultivators and are also quite often misused for other purposes.[98]

3.11. Principle of Co-operative Credit

The attempt to raise a logical or rational structure of co-operative credit involves programmes of action in three different directions, conceptually, so that the total field of credit was meaningfully analysed and related with relevant aspects of economic activity, organisationally, in terms of articulation and implementation of the conceptual scheme of at various levels, and financially, in terms of resources for giving effect to the programme based on the scheme and organisation designed for establishing a well-knit universal system of co-operative credit." The continuing need for financial resources of rural co-operatives in India is the result of three elements – (i) the prevention of exploitation, (ii) the investment of fresh resources so as to initiate development, and (iii) the requirement to grow steadily into an integrated system for a developing economy. Now-a-days it is accepted widely that cooperative credit is the only means of banishing poverty of rural farmers. Co-operative credit is the base for all types of co-operatives.

In India, the co-operative credit has been organised under the following features[100] mainly on the Raiffeisen model:

(i) limitation of area for mutual knowledge,
(ii) share of small value,
(iii) permanent indivisible reserve fund,
(iv) loans for productive purposes,
(v) loans only to members,
(vi) credit for S.T., M.T., and LX facilities with suitable instalments for repayment of loans,
(vii) promotion of moral and material advancement both in purchase of agricultural requisites and sale of agricultural production, Prof. D.R. Gadgil's greatest contribution is the crop loan system which is adopted today by PACS and other financial institutions as the only rational system of providing ST agricultural credit to millions of cultivators in India.[101]

The aims of the co-operative credit listed by Prof. Horace Belshow before the International Conference on Agricultural and Co-operative Credit in 1952 are as under:

1. To promote thrift for increasing supply of funds.
2. To obtain additional resources from outside the society.
3. To promote the effective use of loans and to reduce risk in granting loans by careful and continuous supervision.
4. To reduce the lending risk of credit co-operatives by adequate surety.
5. To keep the cost of credit as low as possible.
6. To endeavour to make societies credit-worthy so that they can obtain sufficient funds to help finance other co-operative undertakings.

However, co-operative credit has been criticised for the manner disbursing the credit, the amount, and the recovery system of the credit. D.G. Karve has rightly remarked that, "only lending money to farmers under co-operative regulations cannot be defined as an activity, contributing to economic development."[102] To make credit effective, a well-developed extension service, supported adequately by research centres and operated closely with the co-operatives for improved agricultural requisites and implements is essential. The adequate and timely credit should be available both for production and consumption needs of the farmers.

3.12. Principles of Better Credit

Various studies have concentrated on the principles of agricultural credit. The principles differ from country to country. S. Nakkiran[103] has given a few cannon of good credit, *i.e.* adequacy, proximity, reasonable rate of interest, supervision and self-management. Timely disbursement of credit is another significant cannon in view of the seasonal nature of agriculture. The provision of better credit operation depends upon national policy and the urge of the credit for agricultural development, and the stage of development that a nation has achieved. Sometimes, the availability of better credit depends upon the institutional or non-institutional agencies engaged in agricultural finance. According to Sir Fredrick Nicholson, co-operative provide 'good credit' to the farmers, because they can mobilise rural savings, promote national thrift, prudence of self-control, arouse new ideas in the general population, of self and mutual help, remove the isolation, the suspicious exclusiveness of the farmers by the benefit of association and suggest new departures in their hitherto conservative methods of cultivation. According to him a simple procedure for acquiring loans is another important principle for Indian situation where majority of farmers are illiterate.

The rural credit survey committee[104] emphasised the following main requirements of institutional system of rural credit:

1. It should be associated with the policies of the state.
2. It must be an effective alternative to the private agency of credit.
3. It should have the strength of adequate resources and well trained agencies of credit.
4. The system has to be coordinated not only internally in relation to the different institutional sectors, pertaining to ST, MT and LT credit, but also with complementary institutional arrangements for making, processing and other economic activities of the cultivator.
5. While providing adequately for essential items of consumption, its main concern should be with loans for production.
6. The period and rate of interest of different types of loans should be related to the purpose which they borrowed.
7. The type of security should be such that, as large a number of solvent producers as possible can avail themselves of credit on the basis of such security.
8. A large part of the credit should be advanced to the producers on the strength of their anticipated crops.
9. The credit agency should be in a position to co-ordinate its activities with those of all the important institutional agencies including Government.
10. It should also be one which can disburse its credit in a positive and constructive way and constantly has in mind the borrower's legitimate needs and interests.
11. It should exist in the village in some form of association of producers who borrow.

To achieve the above requirements, co-operative way is the only institutional approach available. Moreover, co-operative movement allows the poor class to improve their conditions. And majority of poor are the rural poor belonging to agriculture and allied sector. That is why our late Prime Minister Mr. Pandit Jawaharlal Nehru once stated, "we want to include every villager in the co-operative, whether he has resources or not. Unless we do so, only those who have function, others who have not, will not have a chance to go ahead." Regional seminar for Asia on Agricultural Credit for small farmers, Bangkok (Thailand) Oct. 1974 has given certain criteria for suitability and viability of credit system as under:[105]

1. All credit needs (ST, MT, LT) should be met.
2. Credit facilities must he as near the step door as possible when needed.
3. The credit system should be able to generate savings and accelerate economic growth.
4. The system should be capable of achieving compromise between plan objective and differing group interest *i.e.* farmers, credit institutions and govt.
5. The credit system should encourage borrowers to adopt new technologies.
6. Supply of other complementary services should be made.
7. It should be geared to financing the entire farming system.
8. Lending machinery has to match recovery machinery.
9. It should have inter-links with marketing to ensure full recovery etc. Further the seminar also emphasised the necessity to have a system with vertically and horizontally integrated structure of co-operatives.

Long-term credit has a special characteristic which aims at loans for development purposes, and which must be prudently administered. The present LDBs have been adopting rational ways of LT loans for agricultural purposes. These loans are effectively supervised and timely recovery is insisted upon. In this regard the Royal Commission emphasised managerial efficiency and further suggested that no step forward should be taken unless management is efficient. Thus microlevel development credit should improve productivity of land or farm unit. Similarly at macro-level it should result into increase in agricultural output and lead to optimum returns on capital invested.

It therefore, follows that the credit which the agriculturist gets, "must indeed be cheap and facile in that it shall be ever at hand, but it must be credit which shall only be so obtained as it shall educate, discipline and guide the borrower, it should be granted only to those who have learned to think, to plan, to save, the method of providing it must teach the lessons of self and mutual help, and suggest the extension of those lessons to matters outside of mere credit; it must be safe not merely in eliminating the dangers of usury, but in being controlled, heedful and productive. It is emphatically not the mere outpouring of cheap capital that is required nor the mere grant of cheap facile credit to classes unprepared for the boon, what is wanted is the promotion of facilities for saving, the encouragement of banking deposits, the inculcation of the true object, uses and limits of credit, in other words the development of the essential national virtues of thrift, foresight and self-help through institutions organised for those ends."[106]

The best characteristic of the agricultural credit ought to be that it should be safe, cheap and should be available whenever it is demanded. However, credit disbursement should not be a continuous process. During the initial stages, its work is desirable, after a certain stage credit may be neglected, because agriculturists must not require credit. They should have their own funds for the further investment in agriculture. But credit agencies supplying finance to agriculture may face crisis. Therefore, credit is a delicate instrument, which should be managed carefully.

Notes and Reference

1. Report Regarding the Possibility of Introducing Land and Agricultural Banks in the Madras Presidency, p. 46.
2. Nelson A.G. and Murray W.G., Agricultural Finance, Iowa State University Press, Ames Iowa, USA, 5th Edition, 1967, p. 4.
3. *Ibid.*, p. 4.
4. Mellor J.W., Economics of Agricultural Development, Cornell University Press, Ithaca New York, 3rd edition 1968, p. 314
5. Singh S.S., Co-operative for Agricultural Development, University of Jodhapur 1968 has defined agricultural growth, as quantitative increase in the size of total agricultural output

brought exclusively by increasing the quantity of various agricultural inputs (and not through improving their quality).

6. *Ibid.*, defined agricultural development as structural and transformation of pseudo production function of the agriculture by one which is qualitatively better than the existing one.
7. *Ibid.*, defined agricultural progress as connoting equitable distribution, avoiding the downward fluctuation and inducing upward trend in the total agricultural production.
8. Report on Risk and Uncertainty in Agriculture, Chicago.
9. Choubey B.N., Principles and Practices of Agricultural Finance, Asia Publishing House, 1968, p. 63.
10. Fiedler Edgar R. and assisted by Pech Maude R., Measures of Credit Risk and Experience, National Bureau of Economic Research, New York, General Series, 95, p. 5.
11. *Ibid.,* p. 5.
12. *Ibid.,* p. 37, 38.
13. Nelson A.G. and Murray, W.C., *op. cit.,* p. 189-190.
14. *Ibid.*, p. 93.
15. Johl, S.S, and Moore, C.V., Essential of Farm Financial Management, Today and Tomorrow Printers and Publishers, New Delhi, 1970, p. 88.
16. Singh, B.K. and Nautiyal, J.C., An Empirical Estimation of Risk in the Application of Chemical Fertilizers in HYV of wheat and paddy in different regions of U.P., IJAB, Vol. 4, No. 2, April/June 1986.
17. Berry, Peter J. and Robinson Liden J., Portfolio Theory and Financial Structure: An application of analysis, Agricultural Finance Review, Vol. 47, 1987.
18. Penson, Johan B. Jr., Evaluating Financial Trend in Agricultural & Financing Review Vol. 47, 1987.
19. Berry, Peter J. and Robinson Liden J., Portfolio Theory and Financial Structure: An application of equilibrium analysis, Agricultural Finance Review, Vol. 47, 1987, p. 18.
20. Nelson, A.G., Credit as a Tool For Agricultural Producer, N. Cent. Reg. Publ. No. 4 and Great Plains Agricultural Council, Publi. No. 15, 1957, p. 10.
21. Jain, S.C., Management in Agricultural Finance, Vora and Co., Publishers Pvt. Ltd., Bombay, 1970, p. 13-33.
22. Choubey, B.N., Institutional Finance for Agricultural Development, Subhad, Sarswat Pune, 1977, p. 14.
23. Rajagopalan, V., Farm Liquidity and Institutional Financing for Agricultural Development UAE, Vol. XXIII, No. 4, Conference 199, Number Oct-Dec., 1968, p. 26.

24. *Ibid.*, p. 27.
25. Financing Agriculture, Vol. XV, No. 1, Jan/March 1983, p. 37.
26. Nicholson Fredrick — Report on Rural Indebtedness, p. 290.
27. H.P. Prakash Rao, Viability of Rural Branches of Commercial Banks: An Analysis — 10th Economists' Meet, Vijaya Bank, 1987, p. 71-73.
28. *Ibid,* p. 74.
29. Parulekar, A.V. and Ullal, R.S., Branch Banking and Profitability — 10th Economists' Meet, Vijaya Bank, 1987, p. 68, 69.
30. *Ibid.*
31. *Ibid.*
32. Naidu, Tirupati V., Farm Credit and Co-operatives in India, Vora and Co. Publishers Pvt. Ltd., 1968, p. 85.
33. *Ibid.,* p. 82.
34. Govt. of Maharashtra — Manual of Loaning, M.S. Co-op. L.D.B. Ltd., Bombay, 1984, Appendix-B.
35. RBI — Report on Trend and Progress of Banking in India 1983-84.
36. Choubey, B.N., Institutional Finance for Agricultural Development, *op. cit.*, p. 61.
37. Norton, L.J., Financing Agriculture, The Interstate Danville Illionois, 2nd edition, 1948, p. 111-123.
38. Desai, S.M. and Desai, D.K., Farm Production Credit in Changing Agriculture, IIM, Ahmedabad, 1971, p. 79.
39. Bohlen, J.M. and Beal, G.M., Sociological and Socio-Psychological Factors in Capital and Credit Needs in a Changing Agriculture (ed) Baum E.L.D., Diessin, H.G. and Heady, E.O., Capital and Credit Needs in Changing Agriculture, the Iowa State University Press, Iowa. USA, 1961, p. 29.
40. Baum, E.L.D., *et. al.* (ed) *op. cit.,* p, 124.
41. S.C. Jain, *op. cit.,* 1970, p. 149, 150.
42. Norton, L.J., *op. cit.,* p. 3,
43. Anantha, S. Rao & M.N. Dandekar — Non-monetary Transaction Costs of Formal Credit Institutions - An Empirical Study, SBI Monthly Reviews, Vol. XXVIII, No. April, 1989.
44. Norton, L.J. *op. cit.,* p. 3.
45. A.I.R.C.R.C, 1969, p. 69.
46. Quoted by Mathur, B.S. Development Banking in India, National Publishing House, New Delhi, 1974, p. 10, 11.
47. NCDC — Report on Co-ordination of S.T., MT and LT Credit, 1964, p. 12,13.

48. *Ibid.*, p. 11, 12.
49. The Royal Commission Commission on Agriculture, 1928, p. 465.
50. Duggan, I.W. and Battles, R.U., Financing the Farm Business, John Willy and Sons, INC, New York, 1960.
51. Desai, S.S.M., Rural Banking in India, Himalaya Publishing House, 1979.
52. Bhat, M.L., Diversion of Long Term Agricultural Finance, University of Allahabad, 1969, p. 3.
53. P.E.O. Planning Commission — Study of Utilisation of Co-operative Loans, 1965, p. 77.
54. Bhat, M.L., *op. cit.*
55. Lele, Uma, Role of Credit and Marketing Functions in Agricultural Development. IBRD, 1972, I.E.A. Conference Papers, p. 1.
56. Govt. of India (Deptt. of Revenue and Banking), Banking Wing — Report of the Expert Committee on Consumption Credit, April, 1966.
57. The General Report of the Committee of Direction, AIRCS, p. 214.
58. Report of the Crop Loan Evaluation Committee, Part-1, Bombay State Cooperative Bank, Bombay, 1958, p. 53.
59. Herald, G., Contemporary Reading in Agricultural Economy, p. 339.
60. Royal Commission on Agriculture, 1928, p. 465.
61. Darling, M., The Punjab Peasant in Prosperity and Debt. Cumberlege, Oxford University Press, 1947, p. 175, 176.
62. Nakkiran, S., Role of Co-operation in the Dynamic Economy — Co-operative News Digest, Vol. XXIII, Sept. 1972, No. 9, p. 136.
63. A.I.R.C.S.C - Report, Vol II, 1954. p. 162.
64. Choubey, B.N., *opt. cit.*, p. 46, 47.
65. Tardy Luis, Reports of Systems of Agricultural Credit and Insurance, League of Nations, 1938, p. 35,
66. Sharma, S.J. and Prasad B., An Assessment of Production Credit Needs in Developing Agriculture, IJAE, Oct. Dec. 1971, p. 511.
67. International Confederation of Agricultural Credit, Tunis, Tunisia, Oct. 1965
68. Jain, S.C, *op, cit.,* p, 38.
69. Nelson, A.G. and Murray, Agricultural Finance, Iowa State University Press, Ames, Iowa, USA, 5th edition, 1967, p, 93-218.
70. Johl, S.S. and Moore, C.V., Essentials of Farm Financial Management, Today and Tomorrows Printers and Publishers, New Delhi, p. 55-90, 1970.

71. *Ibid.*, p. 63.
72. Dadichi, C.L., Overdues in Farm Co-operative Credit — A Study of Rajasthan, Popular Prakashan Pvt. Ltd., Bombay, 1977, p. 28-30.
73. Desai, B.M. and Desai, D.K., Farm Production Credit in Changing Agriculture, IIM, Ahmedabad, 1971, **p.** 74.
74. Johl, S.S. and Moore, C.V., *opt. cit,,* p. 78.
75. *Ibid,* p. 89.
76. Banerjee, P.K., Indian Agricultural Economy, Financing Small Farmers, Chetna Publications, New Delhi, 1977, p. 165.
77. Vaikunth, Mehta N.I. of Co-operative Management — Supervision of PACS — Report of Field Study in Maharashtra, Gujarat and Mysore.
78. Digby, Margarate, The World Co-operative Movement, Hutchinson, University Library, London, 1965, p. 82.
79. Jain, S.C., *op. cit* p. 138.
80. Gadgil, D.R., Co-operative Finance in India: Some problems.
81. V. Mehta, MI. of Co-op. Management — Supervision of PACS: Report on Field Study in Maharashtra, Mysore, and Gujarat, p. 2.
82. Maclagan Committee Report, 1915.
83. Brossard, Dario B., Supervised Agricultural Credit Combined with Co-operatives and Agricultural Extension in Agricultural Co-operative Credit in Southeast Asia, ICA, 1967, p. 29.
84. *Ibid.*, p. 39-40.
85. F.A.O. (VS) Bangkok—Credit Problems of Small Farmers in Asia and Far- East, 1957, p. 18, 19.
86. General Report of Committee of Direction, A.I.R.C.S., p. 213.
87. Chowdhari, T.P.S. and Sharma, J.N., Crop Loan System: A Study of Andhra Pradesh and Punjab NICD, Hyderabad, p. 7.
88. Choubey, B.N., *op. cit.*
89. Quoted in Wolff, Henry W., People's Bank — A Record of Social and Economic Success, Longmans, Green and Co. 1893, p. 21.
90. Gadgil Committee 1944, R.G. Saraiya Committee 1945, Bombay Co-operative Bank Ass. 1946, Agricultural Credit Organisation (Nanavati) Committee 1947.
91. Desai, Vasant, A study of Rural Economics, Himalaya Publications, 1983, p. 489.
92. Dalaya, C.K. and Sabnis, R.S., Co-operation in Maharashtra: Review and Respective, Centre for the Study of Social Change, 1973, p. 15.
93. Deshpande, V.D. and Padki, M.B., Crop Loan System: A Case Study, Gokhale Institute of Politics and Economics, Poona, Mimeograph series No. 12, 1971.

94. Choubey, B.N., *opt. cit.,* p. 46-47.
95. Shrishrimal, W.C., Co-operative Economy: Problems and Potentialities.
96. Byres, T.J., The Dialectics of India's Green Revolution, South Asia Review, Vol. 5, No. 2, Jan. 1972, p. 99-116.
97. Singh, H and Kalhan, A.S., A Study of Credit Requirement and Advances to Farmers in Patiala District, IJAE Oct-Dec. 1971, p. 447-449.
98. Schiller, Otto M., Co-operation and Integration in Agricultural Production, Asia Publishing House, Bombay, 1969, p. 57.
99. Gadgil, D.R., A Speech on Co-operation, in Writing and Speeches of D.R. Gadgil, Gokhale Institute of Politics and Economics, Pune, Orient and Longman Ltd., 1975, p. 100.
100. Choubey, B.N, *op. cit,* p, 38-39.
101. Datey, C.D., Prof. Gadgil's Contribution to Co-operative Movement, Cooperative News Digest, Vol. XXIII, July 1972, No. 7, p. 8.
102. Karve, D.G., Failure and Success in Indian Co-operative Movement — 3rd Int. Congress on Co-op. Research, Morbourg/ Lahh, 1960.
103. Nakkiran, S., *op. cit.*, p. 136.
104. A.L.R.C.S.C, Vol. II (1954), p. 162.
105. Report on the Working Group (Kamath Committee), R.B.O. April, 1978, p. 15.
106. R.B.I., ACD — Co-operative Village Banks, RBI, Bulletin No. 7. Bombay, 1937, (Ambegonkar and Nanavati), p. 25.

4
Co-operative Village Banks

4.1. Introduction

The co-operative village banks henceforth referred to as CVBs, have been advised to improve the functioning of the agricultural credit needs of rural India. Rural area *vis-a-vis* agriculture has a special characteristic, which should be emphasised in developmental planning strategy. Our co-operative movement has apparently aimed to achieve the goal of integrated rural development. During the last eight decades the movement has quantitatively achieved the major goal but has failed to bring qualitative change.

Agricultural credit was the initial major thrust of the co-operative movement in India. It has the roots in the occasional rural needs raised so far. The development of other than co-operative movement widened and spread in all aspects of life during the period. The major share of co-operative credit in the total institutional credit disbursement is declining, while the share of commercial banking is increasing. Initially commercial banks were not interested in agricultural lending. After their nationalisation the ratio of agricultural lending is increasing. Due to the compulsion of the Govt. policy, they initiate in agricultural lending, but they are unable to fulfil the rural needs. B. Shivaraman Committee[1] explored the fact that, "the commercial banks are not fully accustomed to deal with rural household, the latter are also not familiar with the ways of banks." The share of non-institutional lending is still high even when we have a bank for every 13,000 people. The share of non-institutional credit is about 38 per cent in rural area and 40 per cent in urban area.[2] Besides, the co-operative credit societies and commercial banks are competing with each other in agricultural lending, where the co-operative credit societies are on the verge to be closed. The village adoption scheme of commercial banks under 20-point programme have brought the cooperative credit turnover at a very low level. Even the loaning programmes and the subsidies for people below poverty line are made favourable to commercial banks. The savings from rural areas are harnessed by commercial banks which the co-operatives have failed to mobilise them. Even most of the NABARD funds go to the commercial banks. Shivaraman Committee feels that PACS should immediately take steps for buildup deposit. They will have to adopt an approach and a system that will bring confidence to the rural saver and the potential depositor, of the society or not. After some years this will result into the closure of unviable credit societies first and then viable credit societies slowly. And the elements in co-operation with vested interest in the present set up are reluctant to change the hierarchy of the co-operative credit structure so far accepted since decades ago. Only a symptomatic treatment and postponing or avoiding the problem will not be of any use. Only a social revolution will pave the way for new things and structures. But before that, there can be a solution in the Village Co-operative Banks (CVBs). The viability and economics of CVBs is explained in the corresponding topics, And the concept is analysed on the basis of a study conducted in a tehsil, Shirol (Dist. Kolhapur of Maharashtra State).

4.2. The Urge

B. Shivaraman Committee emphasised that, the banking in rural sector has been in tune with the social and economic environment in which the rural people live and credit institutions have to be innovative and have to devise their policies, procedures and overall approach accordingly. It is imperative that the bank officials dealing with rural sector are rural-oriented, preferably recruited locally, so that they can easily identify themselves with local needs and aspiration. Keeping this in mind, the RBI has brought the concept of "Area Approach". The Committee lays emphasis on family-wise approach to identify needs, which is desirable though time-consuming. This could, however, be undertaken village by village, so that the basic work of rural development can be carried out in a phased manner. The CVBs are expected to work as local banking agents of their members, and can instill in their members a strong feeling of responsibilities for the prompt payment of interest and repayment of loans; and can also provide strong incentives to thrift and savings. This is the main objective of the initial co-operative credit societies. At present the PACS are only credit disbursing agents of District Central Co-operative Banks (DCCBs). They only disburse funds received from DCCBs as agricultural short-term and medium term loans. Their work is merely to collect the loan application and disburse the sanctioned loans. If they are converted into CVBs, where the officials belong to the same villages and can approach the members for deposits, the money accumulated through such local savings may be used for the development of the same village, which would incidentally avoid the problem of regionally imbalance in allocation of funds. Besides, the Govt. with a political influence from local leadership permit the urban co-operative banks at village level as a special case. Now-a-days in Maharashtra there is a hazardous crop of urban banks in both urban and rural areas sanctioned on special grounds. And thus we have various credit agencies engaged in lending activities. The multi-agency approach, in a sense, develops a kind of competition among these banks. The entry of the commercial banks in the field of agricultural financing created more problems, than it was expected to solve.[3]

The present PACS have failed to attract rural savings. Moreover, they also have failed to inspire confidence among rural investors, which encouraging thrift and savings was the main aim of co-operative societies. The Banking Commission, 1972 after analysing the alternative sources for agricultural credit, came to the conclusion that under the circumstances prevailing in the country, neither the co-operative banks nor the commercial banks were in a position to shoulder the entire responsibility of providing in an adequate measure the increasing requirements of agricultural credit along with other services necessary for effective utilisation. The co-operative banks can have the necessary structure and their roots in rural areas are deep, coupled with knowledge of local conditions and problems. But they lack adequate resources and higher standard of management efficiency. On the other hand the commercial banks which command huge resources and competent and well trained personnel, have no roots in rural areas and lack the knowledge of local rural conditions and problems. In such circumstances the combination of principles of co-operative credit and commercial banking as CVBs will definitely solve the problems of the present situation facing the co-operative credit movement. "In planning the future of reorganised societies, the aim should be to transform them into a single contact point in the village for all types of credit they should have the capacity to serve other rural producers such as artisans, craftsmen, and agricultural labourers in respect of their economic activities."[4] The CVBs will cover almost entire need of credit requirement of the ruralities. Once primaries are converted into CVBs, cash credit system may be possible to introduce. Particularly CVBs will succeed in allotting cash credit to cash crops such as coconut, coffee, sugarcane, banana, betel vine, grapes etc. We have Land Development Banks as a separate (now they are under NABARD) long-term credit system. They are co-operative because they are registered under Co-operative Societies Act, but they do not collect the savings of rural people. B. Shivaraman Committee recommended that, the PACS should work as agents of L.D.Bs. The combination of short-term (ST), medium term (MT) and long-term (LT) at CVBs is possible if established. According to the pattern suggested by the banking commission 1972, a number of rural cooperative banks were started in the erstwhile composite state of Madras under special scheme for organisation of rural banks. Many of these are still functioning. Alamural Rural Co-operative Bank (Andhra Pradhesh), Tudiyalur Rural Co-operative Bank (Tamil Nadu) etc. are some of the examples, which were established during 1965.

4.3. Brief History

The term Village Bank was first used by Nicholson, in his report of 1895. The deccan riots paved the way to think at agricultural bank for the riots. The condition of the farmers participating in the deccan riots was too bad to lead a normal life, because of their indebtedness. The land-lords and savakars were the major responsible people of the farmer's indebtedness. Mr. Crooks[5] thus elaborately describes the condition of the farmers. "There is perhaps no more pathetic situation in the whole range of human history than to watch these duel, patient masses stumbling in their traditional way along a path which can lead only to suffering, most of them careless of the future, marrying and giving in marriage fresh generations ever encroaching on the narrow margin which separates them from destitution. Anxious statesman peer into the mists which shroud the future and wonder what the end of all this may be." Similar depictions were noted by John Murdoch.[6]

The idea of establishing agricultural banks has been a much discussed subject ever since the deccan riots. The drought situation and the extravagant expenses in the social and cultural activities of the agriculturist resulted into the borrowing from the money-lenders and traders. Their exploitation was the cause of the riots. Sir Wedderburn and Justice Ranade were the first proponents of agricultural banks. During 1892, Govt. of Madras directed Sir Fredrick Nicholson to study agricultural banks in the province. Mr. H. Dupernex[7] supported the concept of village banks as peoples bank. He investigated the fact that, before Schulze Delitsch, Raiffeisen, Luzzatti and Well Emberg, the advantages of association on co-operative lines had been perceived by the great philosopher and Warrior King Fredrick, the Great of Prussia. He grasped the advantages involved in joint responsibility on very much the same lines as those taken by Mr. Thomason, the well-known Lieutenant Governor of the North-Western Provinces, when he upheld the necessity of affirming its principles in the case of joint and undivided village community. By a simple edict Fredrick forced all the nobles owning land in each province of his kingdom, to unite into associations the members of which were collectively responsible for the obligations undertaken by their united body of the benefit of individual members. The institutions he founded are known as the Land Bank of Prussia."[8] F. Nicholson suggested in his very valuable report on Land and Agricultural Bank, "The kind of credit primarily needed by the rioters of this presidency is continuous, small loans for current needs, including maintenance, cultivation expenses, purchase of stock, payment of revenue, rent and the like, and secondly, long-term loans for permanent improvements. Whatever may the necessary additional capital for improvements be, a more pressing and interest need is for cheap and safe credit in current transactions.[9] He further stated that, if the amiable opinion based upon an enlightened perception of the needs of agriculture rather than upon the fact that the ryot's thirst for cheap capital in order to pour it upon the soil was true, if in other words, land improvement hanks were the desiderium of the ryot, if cheap capital were merely sought for actively productive outlays, banks of any sort that would bring cheap capital would satisfy the need, and greater the indebtedness, the greater the productivity and prosperity of the borrowers. But if it is not so, the Indian ryot is no more heedful or eager for agricultural development than his European counterpart, and direct land and agricultural improvement is the last thing for which credit is sought in Europe."[10]

In 1937 a bulletin published by the RBI entitled, Co-operative Village Banks by Ambegaonkar and Nanavati pointed out co-operatives as the best solution for betterment of rural life."[11] Indebtedness, speaking generally has a complex origin, it is due largely to national and personal characteristics coupled with causes exterior to the individual such as laws, social customs, modes of inheritance, seasonal difficulties and the like. CVB, is not for solving the problem of indebtedness but to mobilise the saving and integration of all village activities. The bank which "fulfils at once the requirements of thrift and credit, while promoting in a high degree those qualities which are essential to high national character are the CVBs. They are not formed by capitalists seeking investments for their funds with the hope of earning dividends thereon, and therefore, widening business regardless of the results to the borrower, but are small groups of men, all of the same neighbourhood, who unite their savings, attract capital by their thrift and prudence, and lend the proceeds to themselves on equitable terms for productive use. The leading principles are thrift, self and mutual help, the thriftly prudent and thoughtful unity with the less careful and heedful, and by the indulgence of association induce in them ideas and habits of thrift and heedfulness; money is carefully saved and still more carefully spent; the bank is an association of men each influencing the other in the direction of prudence and productivity, so that the bank satisfies not merely the postulates of proximity and facility, but pre-eminently that of safety."[12]

Once again it is likely to revive the concept of CVBs in place of PACS, PACS may be converted into CVBs.

4.4. Features of CVBs

Rural development in India depends in a major way on the cooperative movement. The co-operative movement and panchayat raj organisations muse go hand in hand. Agriculture which no doubt needs credit, but its complete dependence on external finance is not a good symptom Farm finance is a traditional approach. The rural financial market plays a significant role in solving the credit needs of farm families. The motivation towards saving and mobilisation of savings of rural people should be emphasised. Sir Denzel Ibbetson in his able speech introducing the agricultural bank bill[13] said that, "the Govt. of India fully realised the doubts and difficulties which must attend any attempts to introduce the Raifeissen system into rural India but they also recognised the enormous advantage which would result to the Indian cultivators if, by any means, they could be induced to utilise their confined savings under a system of co-operative credit and so be freed even partially from the necessity of recourse to the professional money-lenders." But today, the difficulties, which hinder the establishment of CVBs are not observed, which were noted in establishing agricultural bank during the beginning of this century. The apex agency *i.e.* NABARD is established after a great debate in 1982.

The CVBs will have certain features which will be observed in them:

1. The special feature of CVBs will be to ensure mobilisation of rural savings. Rural people have small savings from their earnings, which are mostly captured by commercial banking agency. Larger part of savings is harnessed by commercial banks. Thakurdas Committee (1950) report, signifies the rural saving by stating that, "in case of similar people in rural areas the extension of banking facilities should aim at mobilising small savings and also a part of the incomes likely to be generated as a result of public investment in various projects," The very purpose of this statement will be fulfilled through CVBs. It is likely that small and marginal farmers, tenants and

labourers have also been earning higher incomes with some margin for savings but such savings are being distributed among items of consumption and wasteful expenditure. The CVBs will collect such potential savings more effectively as they will have local contacts, and they will be used for issuing loans to agricultural activities. Agricultural credit should be disbursed only through CVBs.

2. The concept of rural co-operative community will be achieved because planning, organisation and management of rural economic activities will be integrated in such CVBs according to the sources of villages.
3. It will also be helpful in doing away the malpractices in the present set up of PACS. Present structure was to a certain extent helpful in the past, but today the situation has changed. The peoples' expectations from co-operatives are rising and demands of the lower strata of society are increasing. Cooperative principles are fully infused in the living pattern of rural people. These people are now ready for a more advanced way of organising provision of rural credit.
4. The CVBs will work like money-lenders, whenever any financial need arises, it will have to be fulfilled by CVBs.
5. Lending at low rate of interest is possible through CVBs.
6. Integration of short, medium and long term credit through CVBs is possible.
7. The economics of agriculturists may be identified through their 'Khate Book' accounts and transactions with CVBs; this assessment is a complicated affair today.

4.5. Advantages of CVBs

Fredrick Nicholson, who was the principal supporter of CVBs, had clarified some advantages. They are as follows:

1. *Their absolute proximity to the borrower:* The ruralite can borrow the farm finance as and when the need arises. The new approach of rural financial markets will strengthen the money market and also make people save

their income, and enable to strengthen the internal farm finance ratio and investments in farm activities.

2. *Local confidence and local capital:* As local people, involved in CVBs, the confidence in acquiring the funds will psychologically strengthen the attitude and motivation of farmers. Local capital assets may be created by savings and thrifts. The co-operative organisation, in its turn will be helpful to strengthen the confidence and the capital.
3. *Knowledge of borrowers:* A co-operative structure enables the members to know one another. The CVBs will also know their clients intimately as CVBs will be the only guardians of farmers interests. The CVBs will undertake to impart modern knowledge of science and technology related to agriculture, because the welfare of their clients is the welfare of their own. The financial strength will be widened through transactions of CVBs.
4. *Supervisions:* As CVBs will be established in rural area, and the employees serving in CVBs will belong to rural area, they will know the financial assets of each member. Through local contacts and communication the CVBs will have the ability to supervise their lending amount, so as to get it repaid from their clients. Moreover, CVBs will be the only agency which will provide credit to its member farmers.
5. *Cheap credit:* The economics of cheap credit can be prepared CVBs can charge low rate of interest. A cheap and safe credit is essential to farm activities. Once we avoid the intervening agencies between NABARD and CVBs, a low rate of interest is possible. (These agencies, which are essential, should take on administrative functions only.)
6. *Profits within the villages:* Whatever profit the CVBs will earn, will remain with the village, so as to mobilise the funds for welfare activities. Such profits may be lent to the Govt. with the condition that, it should be spent on development activities of the same village/villages area. The rural infrastructure again will thus help to earn more profit, because of its "spread effect".

7. *Agent of member's other activities:* To issue credit and to collect the loans will not be the only business that will be expected from CVBs. The member's interest should be ensured and guided by CVBs. The CVBs will entertain almost all economic, social and cultural activities of the member. It will work as a friend, philosopher and guide of rural people.
8. *Village granaries:* The village level co-operative granaries can be established through the leadership of CVBs. The problem of storage in rural area is serious. Vertical and horizontal integration of co-operative agencies is possible through CVBs. The rural level go downs on co-operative basis, will strengthen the co-operative movement and rural economy of India.
9. *Unity and integrity:* The CVBs will help to unite and integrate the local human and capital resources for the welfare of their own. The aims of national integration can be fulfilled through CVBs. Unity and integrity are indeed an infrastructure for socio-economic development of our country.

4.6. Area of Operation

These villages which have a population of about 5000 or have a cultivated area of about 1000 hectares should have a CVB and in case of a group of villages, which by coming together can fulfil any of the above condition, they should have a joint CVB. This will distribute the CVBs property in village areas.

4.7. Registration

The registration of CVBs will be on the pattern of urban cooperative credit societies. *i.e.,* the registration will be done according to the Co-operative Societies Act. The registration of PACS may be continued.

4.8. Organisation

The CVBs will be located in a village area. The daily work will be carried out on the pattern of daily functioning of a commercial bank. The daily turnover will be recorded by the staff on the patterns of the commercial banks so far adopted. The managerial board of 15 members will supervise the day-to-day functioning of the CVBs. The managerial board will comprise of 10 elected members from among all khatedars in a democratic way and 5 will be co-opted or nominated members from co-operative department, village panchayats, funding agencies, agricultural experts from Govt. departments and a progressive farmer. The board will elect the president and vice-president of the CVBs. The Manager of CVBs will be the member secretary of the Managing Board. The right to vote and elect the managing committee should be available to all khatedars without any conditions.

4.9. Staffing Pattern

Each CVBs will have a staff of four or five employees, *i.e,* a manager, a cashier, one or two clerks, and a peon-cum-saving collector. At present on an average four persons are employed in each PACS, as a Secretary, Asstt. Secretary, helper and a Peon. Therefore, the total number of employees may be roughly the same. In case of higher transactions of CVBs, additional clerks may be added if necessary.

4.10. Salary Pattern

The salaries of employees may be on par with employees of DCCBs. The salary scales vary from one DCCB to another in Maharashtra. However, an employee, should be paid enough satisfied to work in rural atmosphere. The details of this are explained in a case study of Shirol Tehsil. (See 4.18)

4.11. Membership

The socio-economic and cultural impact of PACS, keeps the villages divided into groups. Only certain families or khatedars (landowners) enjoy the membership of PACS, about 50 per cent of Khatedars are deprived of the PACS membership, although the membership is open. "Hundred per cent membership was perhaps the easiest thing which the societies could easily have achieved but which they failed to realise. The reasons are not far to seek. There is, in most of the societies, a dominant, fully entrenched group at the helm of affairs which apart from becoming a dark spot in the progress of co-operative credit expansion has also chosen to become an obstacle against the progress of the rest."[14] All India Rural Credit Survey Committee has emphasised the principles of open membership for all persons residing in the village. On this background, it is felt essential that, all Khatedars must be entitled to be a member of CVB. The CVBs will be permitted to issue loans according to the needs of members and not according to the size of holding for current expenses in agriculture, as a borrower always borrows according to his repaying capacities. The loans for capital investment may be secured," The failure of co-operative credit will always be there as long as attempts are made to the very weak with the very strong. In other words the real problem is only of creating new conditions in which the interests of the weaker are given due protection against the strong."[15] Farmers with large size of holdings borrow larger amounts of loans, which the small farmers can borrow only paltry amounts. Therefore, an attempt should be made to disburse the loans for current expenses of farming on the basis of progress achieved in favour of small farmers. Current expenses include the fertilizers, pesticides, seeds, manures and other maintenance charges and for these purposes the farmers may be given the facility of cash credit. Almost all transactions should be operated through CVBs by a Khatedar, if CVBs are unable to issue credit to the required need of the Khatedars, then the need should be directed to other credit agencies through CVBs, and guarantee of payment should be shouldered by CVBs. All assets owned by a borrower khatedar should be deemed to be pledged to CVBs in case of secured loans. The membership of CVBs in funding agencies should be open. All kinds of *viz.* ST, MT and LT credit should be channelised through CVBs. Such a structure is possible only if solid educational and managerial foundations are laid and appropriate environmental conditions for effective action are created for which certain amendments to the law will have to be passed.

4.12. Finances and Fundings

At present the NABARD is the main funding agent to the cooperative credit hierarchy. The NABARD funds percolate through middle agents like State Co-operative Bank (SCB), DCCBs, PACS, and to agriculturists. The SCBs charge about 2 to 2.5 per cent interest while issuing the loans to DCCBs, and DCCBs charge 2 to 3 per cent more interest while lending the funds to PACS. And again PACS charge another 3 per cent rate of interest high on final lending to the agriculturists. Such rates of interests differ from state to state in India (See Table 4.1).

States/Union Territories	Apex Banks	Central Co-operative Banks	Primary Agricultural Credit Societies
1	2	3	4
			(Per cent per annum)
1. Andhra Pradesh	8.00	10.25	11.50/13.00
2. Assam	10.00/12.00		11.50/14.00
3. Bihar	7.75	9.75	12.50/13.50
4. Gujarat	7.00/7.50	8.00/11.50	9.00/14.00
5. Haryana	7.50	9.50	12.50
6. Himachal Pradesh	10.00		12.50
7. Jammu & Kashmir	7.50	935	11.50
8. Karnataka	7.50/8.15	9.00/11.00	11.50/14.00
9. Kerala	7.50/7.75	9.00/9.50	12.50
10. Madhya Pradesh	7.50/8.00	9.50/11.00	11.50/14.00
11. Maharashtra	7.25	9.00	12.00
12. Manipur	10.00/11.00	*	12.50/15.00
13. Meghalaya	10.25	*	11.75
14. Nagaland	10.50/11.00	*	12.50/13.00
15. Orissa	7.50	10.50	12.50
16. Punjab	7.30	9.00	11.50
17. Rajasthan	7.75	9.00/10.50	11.50/14.00
18. Tamil Nadu	7.66	9.00/10.50	11.50/12.50
19. Tripura	9.75	*	12.50
20. Uttar Pradesh	7.50	9.75	12.50/14.00
21. West Bengal	6.90	9.20	11.00/13.00
22. Andaman and Nicobar	9.35	*	11.35
23. Chandigarh	12.50	*	13.50 to 14.50
24. Delhi	9.50/12.00	*	11.50/14.00
25. Goa, Daman and Din	9.00	*	11.00
26. Pondicherry	9.25/9.75	*	11.50/12.25

Table No. 4.1: Rates of interest charged at various levels of the co-operative credit structure
(As on 30th June 1983) (S.T. agricultural loans)

* There are no CCBs in these areas — Not available.

Source: Study group on Norms for Involvement of Resources by State and Central Co-operative Banks in Agricultural Lending, NABARD, Bombay, 1986, p. 116.

Thus, about 50 per cent interest is charged by these (SCB, DCCB and PACS) middle agencies upon the final borrower of credit on account of administrative charges. If CVBs are established, these middle agencies will be reduced to a minimum and, the result is that the borrower ultimately has to pay about 8 per cent of more interest than what NABARD actually charges.

The farmers will get the benefit of a lower rate of interest, The SCBs should be delinked from the financial hierarchy of co-operative credit structure. Instead of SCBs, state level branches of NABARD may be established. Alternatively, the earlier state LDBs which are- now converted into state Agricultural and Rural Banks may be given such authorities to disburse the all kinds of NABARD loans. The DCCBs as they are well established may be continued to work for development activities separately. And CVBs should get funds directly from NABARD, without any other intermediate agency. In this way the agriculturists may get the relief of about 3 to 4 per cent less rate of interest. The CVBs initially will have to take help from other agencies or at the time of scarce or minor deposits. Once the CVBs are successful in mobilising the rural saving resources there is no need to look anywhere else for help. The agricultural and rural development finances should be disbursed through this hierarchy. If this hierarchy is unable to fulfil the need of rural borrowings, only then the help from commercial banks may be taken. The CVBs should have a freedom to borrow from commercial banks or CVBs should function as guarantee to commercial banks for one who may desire to borrow from commercial banks.

4.13. Conditions of Success

Even with the entry of CVBs, the success of the credit system will depend on the fulfilment of certain conditions such as: (a) an increase in the amount of credit availability, (b) reduction in the cost of credit, (c) adjustment of credit terms to suit the convenience and repayment capacity of the farmers, and (d) provision of assistance in the adoption of suitable modern techniques and improvements in farm management, for which a pilot scheme of CVBs should be launched and then it should be expanded throughout the state. CVBs will provide available credit to the needy farmers, where the need of the farmers is considered instead of credit limit determined by size of holding. Fredrick Nicholson had mentioned the following condition for the success CVBs, as they must take up: (i) whole village life within its ambit, (ii) include everyone in the village, (iii) must be of greater adherence to essential co-operative principles, (iv) must have constant dealings and continuous touch with the members, (v) concentration of a few selected areas should be aimed at rather than wide multiplicity and diffusion. Rural Credit Review Committee recommended credit availability according to the requirements of the farmers rather than on the basis of arbitrary ceiling. Secondly, the cost of credit will be minimised through direct credit from NABARD. And it will be possible to issue (from NABARD) some final loans at lower rate of interest for specific size groups, generally belonging to marginal and small farmers group. But what is required is a confidence and a sense of belongingness instead of vested interests in co-operative movement.

4.14. Vertical and Horizontal Linkages

If the farmers are persuaded to sell their produce through marketing co-operatives the CVBs will have recovery links. The CVBs should be linked to marketing, processing, dairies, service and other co-operatives concerned for the effective repayment and building healthy and wealthy co-operative movement in the country. Borrower khatedars must sell to and borrow from co-operative enterprises. Co-operative principles in Maharashtra combined freedom and independence of the individual with the normal economic advantages of large scale production. Besides the co-operation in Maharashtra has emphasised both horizontal and vertical links. It is horizontal in the sense that, "the number of dependent economic units (in their capacity as buyers and sellers) come together for the discharge of function"[16] and it is vertical in the sense that, "a co-operative is not an independent economic unit, the function it discharges is fully integrated with the economy of each members unit and that alone provides the economic basis for the operation of the co-operative enterprises."[17]

4.15. Khatedar Books

Issuing of khatedar book has become a legal necessity since the last few years in Maharashtra but this has very limited significance. Once they are issued, necessary changes are not made in it. These khatedar books may be used as khate books or land ownership account books of members of CVBs. The size of holding, cropping pattern and quality of soil, fertility, whether the land is irrigated or non-irrigated may be entered in this khate book. The number and names of family members may also be entered in it, with their occupations. The loans and deposits accounts be regularly entered in such books. On, the basis of this book only, a CVB may issue crop loans. No additional certificate should be necessary.

4.16. Stabilisation Arrangements and Subsidies

The stabilisation arrangements to avoid overdues should be made through developing a fund. The CVBs will help to avoid the present problem of overdues in PACS. As regular banks, members will have a better banking facility, which will solve the problem of overdues, which at present are protected by local politics and groups in village. Besides, special credit facilities should be provided to small farmers. Govt. funds and subsidies should directly reach the CVBs through which such facilities will be provided to small and marginal farmers. The loans to agricultural labourers and rural artisans given by CVBs should be guaranteed by labour co-operative societies.

4.17. Training and Education

To strengthen efficiency in management of CVBs training and educational facilities should be made available to the officials of CVBs. Higher and lower diploma courses of co-operative training college (District Co-operative Boards and Regional Co-operative Training Colleges) and Agricultural Banking Colleges and staff colleges of RBI should be obtained by officials concerned. Before implementation of the CVBs such pool of qualified staff may be created through training and education with a planned time-table of training of the present PACS employees. The present management of PACS is incompetent and prone to malpractices. In almost all villages common people take it for granted that PACS is a place of fraud, exploitation and political activity. Though majority of members of PACS are averse to such deviations and mismanagement in PACS, they are generally supported by political influences of district and state level leadership. It is therefore, very essential to keep it totally away from politics. Except the menial staff, the services of all other employees should be transferable at a state level. The menial personnel should be transferable at the district level.

4.18. A Case of Shirol Tehsil

Shirol Tehsil has 50 villages, 58 PACS and two Primary Land Development Banks. The total number of CVBs if categorised according to the strategy, specified earlier will be 34, one CVB for each for 22 village and 12 group CVBs for 28 villages. In these group of CVBs, two villages will have one CVB, one group of three villages will have four CVBs and one group of two villages will have seven CVBs. According to the strategy suggested for staffing pattern suggested the total number of employees required for these 34 CVBs will be 136. At present the tehsil has 85 full-time employed persons in PACS and another 169 full-time employed in other allied activities, who will work even after establishment of CVBs. About 51 persons may get additional job opportunities if PACS are converted into CVBs.

The salaries of employees should be as follows:

Manager	–	₹ 1500	p.m.
Cashier	–	₹ 1400	”
Clerk	–	₹ 950	”
Peon	–	₹ 950	”
Total	–	₹ 4750	”

The total salary expenditure of each CVB will be ₹ 4750 p.m. The total expenditure of all (34) CVBs will be ₹ 16,500 per month, and the yearly salary expenditure of all CVBs will be ₹ 19,38,000. At present all employees of PACS in Shirol taluka earn ₹ 11,70,319 as annual salary. If PACS are converted into CVBs, certain amount of expenses will be saved. Similarly the profits from the margin between the rates of interest on deposits and loans will be high, which will be compensated for higher expenses on account of salaries. In short

CVBs are possible on the same level of expenses as in the case of PACS. But the efficiency and effectiveness will increase, which will bring qualitative change in rural development. According to the survey conducted for doctoral dissertation,[18] the average per family net saving was ₹ 650 during 1984-85. If this proportion is assumed and applied to the whole tehsil, the total savings in a taluka will stand at ₹ 234 crores. This amount is sufficient enough to function the CVBs efficiently.

4.19. Conclusions

The suggestions regarding CVBs deserves careful consideration and acceptance as a way of proper integration of both commercial and co-operative principles. The impact of co-operative movement on the national economy is quite substantial, so far as capital accumulation is concerned. In Western Europe and North America, the co-operatives have attracted huge sums by way of deposits from members and have invested these in productive and income generating undertakings. We have, so far missed this vital opportunity of achieving greater mobilisation of local resources for local development of a self-financing nature. As Nicholson had rightly said, "it is not in great schemes or institutions, not even in specially granted privileges, that success lies, but in unassuming labours, which starting with simple ideas, simple aims and simple facts overcome each difficulty as it arises, and perfect the systems which shall be found suitable to the need of the country. Success can only arise from the long, continuous efforts of zealous men who while informed in the details of every method, yet tried, can yet live along the people, vivify them with their own spirit and intelligence, energise them with some of their own enthusiasm, and with them, work out in actual fact, even though on the humblest lines," a practical programme of improvement.

Notes and References

1. R.B.I. (B. Shivaraman), Report of the Committee to Review Arrangements for Institutional Credit for Agriculture and Rural Development, 1981, p. 30.
2. 37th Round NSS. No. 322 and Some Aspects of Indebtedness of Rural and Urban Households, GOI, New Delhi, 1985.
3. Shrishrimal, W.C., *op, cit.* 1978, p.

4. B. Shivaraman Committee, RBI, 1981, p. 360.
5. Quoted in Murdoch John, Inadequacy of Agricultural Banks to Meet the Needs of India, A Supplementary Measure Absolutely Necessary, The Christian Literature Society for India, 1903, p. 1.
6. *Ibid.*
7. Dupernex, H., People's Bank for Northern India: A Handbook to the Organisation of Credit on a Co-operative Basis, Thacker Spink and Co., 1900.
8. *Ibid.,* p. 30.
9. Report on Land and Agricultural Bank — F. Nicholson, Vol. I, p. 15.
10. *Ibid.,* p. 16.
11. Co-operative Village Bank, RBI, ACD, Bulletin No. 2, Bombay, 1937.
12. *Ibid.,* p. 25, 26.
13. Murdoch, John, *op. cit.,* p. 2.
14. Mohite, Y.J., The Co-operative Movement in Maharashtra State: A Reappraisal, Govt. Central Place, Bombay, 1970, p. vi.
15. *Ibid.,* p. xix.
16. Knapp, Joseph R, Co-operative Expansion Through Horizontal Integration, JFE. Vol. 32, No. 4, 1950, p. 1031, 1047.
17. *Ibid.*
18. Jugale, V.B., Socio-Economic and Technological Impact of Co-operative Credit on Agriculture, Shivaji University (unpublished), 1987.

5
Conclusions

Agriculture, no doubt is a task to manage as it is in the hands of illiterate and traditional cultivators. It is a science, which is developing rapidly in various dimensions. The management aspect which is mostly related to land, soil, water, fertilizers, pesticides etc. plays a significant role in farm activities. The cultivator has to think, decide about and manage farm activities according to the prevalent circumstances and factors of production. The traditional practices are made known to the entrants in the sector and they continue generation after generation. But now-a-days science has entered in each and every field of human activity and thus a drastic change has been brought in the agricultural practices. Today an illiterate farmer without any skills cannot practise agriculture. Till today a person who cannot get a job in tertiary sector and has sufficient land to carry out the agri-business remains in the sector. But in future he cannot survive in agriculture without technological know-how. And the fact is that second generation of agriculturists are reluctant to involve themselves in this sector, because of rising input costs and decreasing yield.

A farmer has to understand nature (climate, soil, possibility of rain, summer, winter, etc.) and then he has to manage the farm according to his family needs. A decision-making process in agricultural activities is so significant that it has to be dealt with. So, a farmer manager has to integrate various managerial aspects like, tillage, soil, land, water, crop, weeding, intercultures, harvesting marketing, etc. His task is more difficult than that of an industrial manager, because industrial sector is in the hands of highly trained and talented executive and bureaucrats.

The entrepreneurship in farm activities is different from industrial entrepreneurship. An indigenous farm management science should be developed instead of following on the western line. The human resource development in farm-activities is more significant than material or physical development.

Farm finance is one of the major capitals (both fixed and variable) *input* used since time immemorial. When farmers have to borrow external credit they have to manage it very carefully, because repayment of loan should become easy. Lending agencies always protect their interests, while borrower is entirely at the mercy of nature. So, restructuring of financing institutions particularly PACS at the grass- root level is essential because our farmers have great faith in the cooperative movement. And the movement is held responsible to bring socio-economic changes in some part of our country. Co-operative Village Banks will definitely bring new enthusiasm in the rural farm community. The real success of co-operative movement depends upon micro-level achievements of the societies, which are being recommended to be converted into CVBs. If the grass-root level agencies are made strong, the co-operative movement will be strong and if they are weak the movement will become weak. Through co-operative village banks, it is possible to build such a co-operative credit system which will cover: (i) the risk and uncertainty of both lenders and borrowers, (ii) the credit supply according to the need of the agriculturists, (iii) both business, moral and social aspects of the organization, (iv) reduction in cost of borrowing, (v) wider scope for consumption loans, which are actually not unproductive, (vi) both the kind and cash loans, (vii) mobilization of small savings and creation habit of thrift among ruralites, (viii) a need to vitalise the MT loans.

CVBs as a social association can also be effective in bringing about improvement in the sodo-cultural and socio-economic conditions of the ruralites. Moreover, farmers may be motivated to prefer the LT credit which is development credit, prudently administered, effectively supervised and linked to the repayment. To encourage female participation is an aspect to be developed simultaneously, by providing certain incentives.

Therefore, rural credit system should be restricted and reorganized for further consolidation of economic gains and confidence obtained by the rural and female population.

Select Bibliography

Baum, E.L.D. Diessin, H.G., Heady, E.O. (ed) — Capital and Credit Needs in Changing Agriculture, the Iowa state- University Press, Iowa, USA., 1961.

Bhat, M.L. — Diversion of Long Term Agricultural Finance, University of Allahabad, 1969.

Banarjee, P.K. — Indian Agricultural Economy; Financing Small Farmers, Chetna Pub., New Delhi, 1977.

Choubey, B.N. — Principles & Practices of Agricultural Finance, Asia Pub. House, 1968.

— Institutional Finance for Agricultural Development, Shubhada Sarswat, Pune, 1977.

Chowdhari, T.P.S. & Sharma, J.N. — Crop Loan Systems: A Study of Andhra Pradesh & Punjab, NICD, Hyderabad

Catanack. I.J. — Rural Credit in Western India: Rural Credit and Co-operative Movement in Bombay Presidency, 1875-1930, University of California Press, 1970.

Dupernex, H. — People's Bank for Northern India: A Handbook to the organisation of credit on a coop, basis, Thacker's Spink & Co., 1900.

Desai, D.M. & Desai, D.K. — Farm Production Credit in Changing Agriculture, IIM, Ahmedabad, 1971.

Duggan, I.W. & Battles, R.U. — Financing the Farm Business, John Willy & Sons, IMC, New York, 1960.

Desai, S.S.M, — Rural Banking in India, Himalaya Pub. House, 1971.

Darling, M. — The Punjab Peasant in Prosperity and Debt, Cumberleg Oxford University Press, 1947.

Digby, Margarate — The World Co-op. Movement, Hutchinson University Library, London, 1977.

Dalaya, C.K. & Subnis, R.S. — Cooperation in Maharashtra: Review & Respective, Centre for Study of Social Changes, 1973.

Deshpande, V.D. & Padki, M.B. — Crop Loan System: A Case Study, Gokhale Institute, Pune, mimeo series No. 12, 1971.

Fiedler, Edge R. & Assisted by Pech, M.R. — Measures of Credit Risk & Experiences, National Bureau of Economic Research, Gen. series-95.

F.A.O.(Vs) Bangkok — Credit Problems of Small Farmers in Asia & Far East, 1957.

Griffins, Keith — The Political Economy of Agrarian Change: An Essay on the Green Revolution, Macmillan, 1974.

Govt. of Maharashtra — Manual of Loaning, M.S. Coop. L.D.B. Ltd. Bombay, 1984.

Govt. of India (Deptt. of Revenue & Banking) — Banking Wing — Report of the Expert Committee on Consumption Credit, 1966.

Gadgil, D.R. — A Speech on Cooperation: In writting & Speeches of D.R. Gadgil, Gokhale Institute, Pune, Orient & Longman Ltd., 1975.

Howse, C.J. — Agricultural Development without Credit, Agricultural Adm. Vol. 1, 1974.

Jugale, V.B. — Socio-Economic & Technological Impact of Cooperative Credit on Agriculture, Shivaji University Ph.D. Thesis, 1987.

Johl, S.S. & Moore, C.V. — Essentials of Farm Financial Management, Today & Tomorrow Printers & Pub., New Delhi, 1970.

Jain, S.C. — Management in Agricultural Finance, Vora & Co. Pub., Bombay, 1970.

Kahlon, A.S. — Modernisation of Punjab Agriculture, Allied Pub., 1984.

Karve, D.G. — Failure & Success in Indian Co-op. Movement – 3rd Int. Congress on Coop. Research, Morborg/Lahh, 1960.

Mosher, A.I. — Getting Agriculture Moving, Agri. Dev. Council, (Fedrick A. Paeger Pub.), New York, 1968.

Mehta, S.C. — Agricultural Credit Mobilisation & Allocation: With Sp. Reference to Dist. Jhabua (M.P.), Vora Pub. & Distributors, Allahabad, 1987.

Mamoria, C.B. & Saksena, R.D. — Cooperation in India, Kitab Mahal, 1983.

Mellor, J.S. — The Economics of Agricultural Development, Cornell University Press, Ithaca, New York.

Mohite, Y.J. — The Co-op. movement in Maharashtra State: A Reprisal, Govt. Central Place, Bombay, 1970.

NSS 37 round No. 332 — Some Aspects of Indebtedness in Rural & Urban Household, 1985.

Naidu, Tirupati V. — Farm Credit & Co-operatives in India, Vora & Co. Pub., 1968.

Nelson, A.G. — Credit as a Tool for Agricultural Production — N. Cent. Reg. Publ. No. 4 & Great Plains Agricultural Councils Publ. No. 15, 1957.

Nelson, A.G. & Moore, W.G. — Agricultural Finance, Iowa State University Press, AMES, Iowa, USA (5th ed.), 1967.

Nicholson, F. — Report on Rural Indebtedness.

Norton, L.J. — Financing Agriculture: The Interstate, Danville Illions (2nd Ed.), 1948.

NCDC Report on Co-ordination of ST, MT & LT Credit, 1964.

P.E.O. Planning Commission — Study of Utilization of Co-operative Loans, 1965.

Report on Risk & Uncertainty in Agriculture, Chicago.

R.B.I. — Co-operative Village Banks A.C.D., Bulletin No. 2, Bombay, 1937.

Report on Land & Agricultural Bank, Vol. I.

Report on the Crop Loan Evaluation Committee, Part-I, Bombay State Coop. Bank, 1958.

R.B.I. — Report of Committee to Review Arrangements for Institutional Credit for Agriculture & Rural Development, 1981.

Shinde, Annasaheb — Seti Va Pani Niyojan Va Dharanasambandhiche kanhi Prashna (Marathi).

Shrishrimal, W.C. — Cooperative Economy: Problems & Potentialities, The M.S.C. Bank, 1978.

Schillar, Otto M. — Cooperation & Integration in Agricultural Production, Asia Pub. House, Bombay, 1969.

The Royal Commission on Agriculture, 1928.

The General Report of the Committee of Direction (A.I.R.C.S.).

Tardy, Luis — Reports of Systems of Agricultural Credit & Insurance, League of Nations, 1938.

Vaikunth, Mehta N.I.C.M. — Cooperation: An Interdisciplinary Approach - proceedings of a seminar, 1969.

— Supervision of PACS — Report of Field Study in Maharashtra, Gujarat & Mysore.

Vijaya Bank — 10th Economists Meet, 1987.

Index